MARCO ⊕ POLO

D1460745

ORWAY

Norwegian
Sea

SWEDEN
FINLAND
NORWAY   RUSSIA
Oslo   Helsinki
Stockholm
Kristiansand   Saint
Petersburg
ESTONIA
LATTVIA
DENMARK   LITHUANIA
RUSSIA   BELARUS
POLAND

The best Insider Tips → p. 4

INSIDER TIP

The South → p. 32

The West → p. 48

Trøndelag → p. 64

SYMBOLS

INSIDER TIP	Insider Tip
★	Highlight
●●●●●	Best of ...
𝇋	Scenic view
☺	Responsible travel: for eco-logical or fair trade aspects
(*)	Telephone numbers that are not toll-free

PRICE CATEGORIES HOTELS

Expensive   over 1000 kroner

Moderate   800–1000 kroner

Budget   under 800 kroner

Price for two in a double room, with breakfast

PRICE CATEGORIES RESTAURANTS

Expensive   over 350 kroner

Moderate   230–350 kroner

Budget   under 230 kroner

The prices are for a meal with a starter, main course and dessert, as well as a soft drink but without any alcohol

On the cover: Picture-postcard scenery in West Norway p. 51 | Beneath the midnight sun p. 108

CONTENTS

Nordland → p. 70

Lofoten → p. 80

Troms → p. 86

Road atlas → p. 130

DID YOU KNOW?
Timeline → p. 12
Local specialities → p. 26
The endless coast → p. 75
Books & films → p. 77
Budgeting → p. 119
Currency converter → p. 124
Weather in Oslo → p. 123

MAPS IN THE GUIDEBOOK
(132 A1) Page numbers
and coordinates refer to
the road atlas
(0) Site/address located off
the map. Coordinates are
also given for places that are
not marked on the road atlas
(U A1) Refers to the Oslo
street map inside the back
cover

**INSIDE BACK COVER:
PULL-OUT MAP →**

PULL-OUT MAP 𝄢
(𝄢 A1) Refers to the
removable pull-out map
(𝄢 a1) Refers to additional
insert maps on the
pull-out map

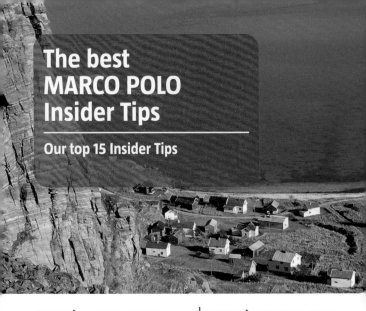

The best MARCO POLO Insider Tips

Our top 15 Insider Tips

INSIDER TIP **Classical music with seagulls in the background**

The Risør Chamber Music Festival combines maritime surroundings with brilliant artistry. A mixture of harbour life, summer resort and classical music on the Skagerrak – when the weather is fine, you will wish that time could stand still → **p. 115**

INSIDER TIP **Relaxing Norwegian-style**

There is a perfect balance between a relaxed atmosphere and choice food which is why it attracts both business people and students. There may be no frills in the Café Opera in Bergen but the dessert is accompanied by music and art → **p. 55**

INSIDER TIP **Tee off into the North Sea**

For the two months of summer, Lofoten Golfbane is the most beautiful golf course on earth – you can tee off looking straight into the midnight sun and the only noise to disturb you will come from the surge of the waves → **p. 108**

INSIDER TIP **A change of climate**

The Jotunheimen Klimapark 2469 is located high up in the mountains 360 km (225 mi) from Oslo. An unknown world was discovered there in a glacier tunnel and definitely proves one thing: it's getting warmer → **p. 35**

INSIDER TIP **With the miners on Spitzbergen**

The former miners' canteen is now the dining room: the polar bears' realm begins just beyond Spitsbergen Guesthouse on Svalbard → **p. 88**

INSIDER TIP **Delectable bread in the fjell**

A first-class Norwegian chef serves the best bread north of the Skagerrak in Bakeriet i Lom → **p. 36**

INSIDER TIP **Perfect Norwegian fjords**

The ship steams from the majestic Sognefjord towards the snow-covered mountains and glaciers – and everybody on the ferry from Balestrand to Fjærland remains on deck → **p. 60**

BEST OF ...

● *Not just white marble*

One of most spectacular (free) views of Oslo is from the roof of the *Operahuset*, the new opera house. This is beautiful at any time but especially spectacular just before sunset when the colours in the sky are reflected in the fjord → p. 44

● *Twisting your way up the coast*

Toll booths may be familiar sights – but not on the *Atlantic Ocean Route*, perhaps the most unusual road to explore in Norway. The road snakes its way along the coast over bridges and islands: you can even fish from lay-bys and the gusts of wind make you think you're at sea → p. 59

● *Monumental art in the park*

Art appreciation with a picnic atmosphere: take your time to admire the famous sculptures in the *Vigelandsparken* and then stroll across to Frøgnerpark, one of the most popular places in the capital for meeting up with friends in the summer → p. 44

● *A hoard of modern art*

You can see one of the largest collections of modern art in Scandinavia without paying in the *Henie-Onstad-Kunstsenter*. You just have to decide to go there on a Wednesday when admission to the Kunstsenter, founded in 1968, is free → p. 42

● *Fortress with a view*

You should not miss out on a view of the Oslofjord from the *Åkershus Fortress*. You have to pay to get into the Palace with the royal mausoleum but you can visit the fortress complex for free → p. 42

● *Lively Hanseatic quarter*

The *Bryggen* harbour district is so beautiful that the people of Bergen should really charge admission. But, seeing that the almost 400-year-old houses are still used as offices, homes, restaurants and cafés, Norway's loveliest open-air museum remains a place where you do not have to pay (photo) → p. 54

● *National pride*

Fresh birch twigs are an essential part of the *Norwegian national holiday* on 17 May, Constitution Day. If you can, try to be in Oslo on that day. The celebrations in the capital are especially charming with a children's procession concluding the festivities → p. 114

● *The more extreme the better*

Thousands battle their way through the forests and over the mountains from Rena to Lillehammer on skis, bikes or even on foot as part of the *Birkebeineren Long Distance Race*. Join in if you feel fit enough: extreme sports are the done thing in Norway! → p. 108

● *Perfect craftsmanship*

The early days of Christianity in Norway have left magnificent reminders of that time: the stave churches with their – partially heathen – decoration. On no account should you miss the famous *Borgund Stavkirke* near Lærdal on the Sognefjord → p. 60

● *The winter sports' experience*

Not interested in ski jumping? You don't have to be to enjoy a visit the *Holmenkollen Ski Jump*. It holds the same place in the hearts of ski-jumpers as the Scala in Milan does with opera buffs. Visit the Ski Museum – and you will be breathless when you see the magnificent view → p. 42

● *Carved out in the Ice Age*

Norway's fjords are the missing link between the coast and the fjell. If you visit one of the most beautiful arms of the sea – the *Lysefjord* near Stavanger – you will see what is above and below, the sky and the water, in a completely new light – literally (photo) → p. 63

● *Epic on the sea*

The surroundings of the *Peer Gynt Festival* on Gålåvatnet Lake are unbelievably beautiful. This is the place for you to see a traditional production of Norway's most famous play. The hero in Henrik Ibsen's dramatic poem is the embodiment of the way Norwegians see themselves: adventurous but narrow-minded, imaginative but absolutely realistic → p. 40

BEST OF ...

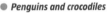

● **Penguins and crocodiles**
Creatures that live in or near the water have found a new home in the *Akvariet* in Bergen. You will not only come across penguins and seals in the aquarium, but also snakes and crocodiles → p. 53

● **Under glass**
The ruins of the cathedral are the main attraction in the *Hedmarksmuseet* in Hamar. The impressive glass pyramid will also protect you from the rain – and give you the opportunity to experience the special atmosphere of the place (photo) → p. 40

● **The treasure in the silver mountain**
2300 exciting metres into the heart of the mountain: the pit railway takes you through the galleries and vaults of the old *silver mine* in Kongsberg → p. 46

● **Hunt, shop, look**
You can outwit the bad weather in the *Devoldfabrikken* in Ålesund. Here, you will not only find the famous Devold pullovers but also many articles made by other sportswear and leisure clothes companies. And then there is the café with a wonderful view of the islands offshore → p. 50

● **The fascination of the fjell**
Mountains near the Arctic Circle are a harsh environment for people, animals and plants to survive – and it was a long way from hunters and gatherers to modern tourists with their high-tech equipment. All of this is shown in the *Norsk Fjellmuseum* in Lom → p. 35

● **Just like the good old days**
Perfectly set tables and the aroma of fresh bread and pastry: *Farmors Stue* in the centre of Bodø is a small café run by generous people with great taste and a friendly welcome! → p. 73

RAIN

RELAX AND CHILL OUT
Take it easy and spoil yourself

CHILL OUT

● *Regal relaxation*
The *Holmenkollen Park Hotel* in Oslo is a fairy-tale palatial hotel with a health spa oasis and unbelievably beautiful view over the capital city and its fjord. Each minute in the hotel, each titbit in the restaurant – pure indulgence and pleasure (photo) → **p. 45**

● *A cruise in an open-air cinema*
You will spend as much time as possible on deck relaxing, reading, taking photos or just watching the scenery. As the ship glides past fjords, peaks and islands, more islets, reefs and skerries appear on the horizon. A trip on one of the *Hurtigruten* ships is like being in a gigantic open-air cinema and is a feast for all the senses → **p. 75**

● *The light of Jæren*
Beautiful beaches, dunes and the murmur of the waves: an arche-typical Norwegian environment awaits you in the *Sola Strand Hotel* south of Stavanger. Swimming pool, sauna and related spa facilities top off this relaxing experience → **p. 63**

● *Over the mountains and down to the sea*
If you are lucky, it will seem like you are on a trip through all four seasons when the train winds its way 1220 m (4000 ft) up into the mountains and passes the huge Hardanerjøkulen Glacier. There can be no doubt that the *railway line between Oslo and Bergen* is one of the most beautiful in Europe → **p. 104**

● *Steam bath in the North Sea*
Let's be honest; the weather in Bodø is fair to middling. But a few hours in the *Nordlandsbadet* with its warm swimming pools, whirlpools, herbal steam bath and sauna will soon bring your body back to operating temperature → **p. 74**

● *A steamer to the slopes*
The Telemark is really a synonym for winter sports. But, you can also discover the sporting region in comfort on board one of the two *old steamers Victoria* and *Henrik Ibsen* → **p. 47**

INTRODUCTION

DISCOVER NORWAY!

Midsummer night somewhere on the coast far north of the Arctic Circle: white sand, blue sea, rocks washed clean by the water and the sun sinking slowly towards the surface of the water on the horizon only to rise again a few minutes later – this would be the perfect picture of the natural phenomenon if it weren't for the clouds or mist which sometimes force their way into the picture.

The people who live in the houses near the beach also know another side to their wild country, too. They use iron chains to anchor their roof trusses to the ground because they know you can't fool around with nature and its fickle moods. After a mild midsummer night, the wind can get up and suddenly fog can chase boats back to port. The sun actually disappears for a couple of hours in summer in Sørlandet, Norway's strip of coast on the Skagerrak, but holiday-makers there still sit together after they have finished their barbeques until dawn breaks, making the most of every moment.

Norway has a great variety of landscapes full of surprises. Gigantic forests conceal lakes and rivers full of fish, the ice of the glaciers towers above the plateaus and the mountains

Photo: The skerres in Sørlnadet

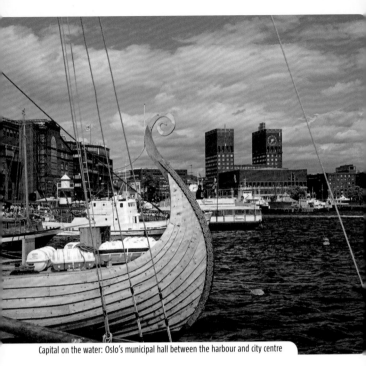
Capital on the water: Oslo's municipal hall between the harbour and city centre

The fjords – An expression of nature's power

are bisected by enormous deep valleys. Thousands of islands are dotted along the coast which is continuously interrupted by the absolutely unique fjords. They are expressions of the power of nature just as the midnight sun and northern lights are. In Norway, new vistas open up around every corner and, if you allow all your senses to be taken over by this country, you will experience something very special: harmony.

8000 BC
At the end of the Ice Age, the first people follow reindeer and other game to the north

7000–4000 BC
Settlement of the Finnmark area. In the south, transition to agriculture

1500–500 BC
Bronze Age. In the south, mainly rural cultural forms; in the north, hunting

793–1066
Viking era

872
Harald 'Beautiful Hair' Hårfagre unites large sections of Norway. The, sometimes bloody, process of consolidation lasts for

It appears that they do things differently in Norway. It may have something to do with the location and specific topography of the country and certainly with the Norwegians' national pride. They decided twice against joining the European Union, and even signing an agreement on a more open marketing policy met with great resistance from the population. The reason could be the wealth that can be found lying beneath the sea on the continental shelf off the coast of Norway. Every year, Norway sells 52 billion pounds (80 billion US$) worth of oil and gas – something like 20 percent of the gross national product. The country's savings account – here it is called The Government Pension Fund – Global – is padded with 328 billion pounds (500 billion US$) and is hardly ever touched. The Norwegians are well aware of their good fortune, and know that the 'black gold' guarantees their wages and puts money into the state's coffers. They are really proud of what their country between the Skagerrak and North Cape has to offer.

In the middle of the 19th century, the poet and linguistic researcher Ivar Aasen wrote *The Norwegian*. It is taught in schools and sung on the National Holiday on 17 May:

Wealth off Norway's coast: oil and gas

"Between hills and rocks, out by the sea. The Norwegian has found his homeland where he has cultivated his own property and built his house with his own hands." Having braved the harsh climate and made the hostile land fertile fills Norwegians with pride. They have the greatest respect for nature. One of the many events of 17 May is the open-air church service on Hardanger-jøkulen – as many as 2000 people hike on their skis to the glacier at an altitude of 1800 m (5900 ft) to take part. In this way, nature becomes a temple.

The beauty of Norway's landscape reveals itself as soon as one gets out of the sprawl of the cities on the southern coast of the country. Nine of the ten largest cities in Norway are located in the area up to Trondheim. The Oslo metropolitan area is home to a good million of Norway's total population of 5 million while only around 10 percent live in the three northern administrative districts (*fylker*). The Kingdom of Norway consists of 19 *fylker* and 435 communities. The smallest is the island of Utsir to the north-west of Stavanger with only 218 inhabitants living in an area of 1500 acres. In Kautokeino in Finnmark, 3000 residents are scattered over 9707 km² (3748 mi²)– more than six times the area of London. Without the arctic island groups of Svalbard

around 200 years	c. 1250	1349–50	1397–1523	1814	1905
	The Hanseatic League establishes outposts and exploits the country	50 to 60 percent of the population fall victim to the Black Death	Kalmar Union (Denmark, Sweden and Norway)	Denmark cedes Norway to Sweden. The Norwegian constitution is passed on 17 May in Eidsvoll	Norway dissolves its union with Sweden

and Jan Mayen, Norway covers an area of 323,364 km² (124.851 mi²), with a population density of 36 people per square mile.

Two thirds of Norway is made up of fjell – mountains and high plateaus – and 37 percent of the country is forested. As only around three percent of the surface is arable, a lot of room is left for leisure activities. On Sundays, the Norwegians go *på tur*, through the woods or up the next mountain, fishing, berry-picking or collecting mushrooms.

> **Two thirds of the country is covered with mountains and high plateaus**

Races are held throughout the country – in summer, in running shoes and on skis in winter. Soon after they start school, Norwegian children are taught how to survive in the great outdoors, how to make a place to sleep without a tent, how to fish and carve and behave responsibly on the water. And in no other country in Europe are there more hunting weapons in comparison to the population than in Norway. From the end of August to late in October, the huntsmen and women hardly have time for anything at the weekends other than stalking reindeer, elk and other animals.

According to the United Nations Development Programme (UNDP), Norway has, for many years, been the country offering the highest quality of life in the world. Factors such as life expectancy, average income and education show that the land of the midnight sun is not a bad place to live in. In spite of all this, many Norwegian want to make more use of the national savings account to reduce the price of food, petrol and alcohol and increase wages and pensions. Another challenge to be solved in the 21st century is the relationship between living in cities and the countryside. Four out of five Norwegians live in towns or large municipalities. The cities are becoming more attractive because they provide better opportunities for work, leisure and culture. The massive tax reliefs provided have not been able to stop the population of the smaller villages in North Norway and on the islands diminishing; jobs and possibilities for work are disappearing. The only hope remaining lies in the Norwegians' deep-rooted love of their country and its traditions. The people do not want to give up what nature has given them or they have created with their own hands. This is a good thing because it would be impossible to get to know this country without its people. They take their time – time to experience and enjoy. Hustle and bustle is only found in cities – and

1940–45
Occupation of Norway by the German Wehrmacht

Mid-1960s
First promising oil discoveries in the North Sea

1972
EU referendum: 53 percent of the Norwegians vote against membership

1991
Harald V crowned king

1994
Second 'no' to EU membership

2010
The Norwegian Oil Fund is valued at 328 billion pounds (500 billion US$)

the Norwegians say that there is really only one of those in the entire country.

In coastal villages, the old people get together to have a chat on the quay – this is almost a ritual for many of them, especially in the morning when the fishing boats come back with their catch. Further inland, it is normally the hikers who strike up a conversation about the weather, surroundings and route. Many holiday-makers have been surprised at how helpful the Norwegians, who are generally considered to be rather reserved, can be. It seems that

The Norwegians take time to enjoy themselves

their restraint only comes from their wish not to annoy other people. The Norwegians from the south are though to be more aloof than those from the north but none of them are impolite. Don't be surprised if, on a lovely summer day, somebody invites you to have a cup of coffee on their veranda or to go for a short boat trip. Let yourself be infected with the feeling that there is always enough time for a relaxed chat that can easily overcome any language barriers.

But, above all, Norway is a paradise for nature lovers and most of the tourists don't come here to go shopping. The are looking for unspoilt nature rather than urban life and have no trouble accepting that there are very few good restaurants and only a limited offer of food outside conurbations.

The coast near Moskenesstraumen on the southern tip of the Lofoten

They want tranquillity and torrential rivers, views and adventure. And the first shock at the high prices soon gives way to the astonishment that the Norwegians have managed to make every corner of their country accessible by road and supplied with electricity. Nowhere will you have to do without your creature comforts. But, if you want to, go ahead – there's more than enough room!

WHAT'S HOT

1 Zany art

Comic Heroes Mickey Mouse is old hat. *Martin Ernsten (www.martinernsten.com)* and *Bendik von Kaltenborn (www. benkalt.no)* are the new heroes of the comic scene. The two imaginative personalities have created something completely new with their comics. Every autumn, cartoonists show what they can do at the Raptus – Bergen Comics Festival *(www.raptus.no)*. The *Outland Kristiansand (Dronningens gate 19, Kritiansand)* and *Aliblabla AS (Bærumsvelen 210, Bekkestua)* comic shops stocks a wide selection.

Icy experience 2

Afraid of heights? Have you ever climbed a waterfall? In Norway, you can. Rjukan is the most popular place in Europe for ice-climbers. You can rent the necessary equipment and book tours from *Rjukan Adventure (Storgata 23)*. The Hydnefossen Waterfall in Hemsedal and the waterfalls near Lærdal also offer superb climbing conditions. This sport is only for experts. The *Norwegian Mountain Hiking Association (DNT, photo)* can provide the knowhow *(Storgata 3, Oslo)*. Upptur also organises tours and offers ice-canyoning excursions that are also suitable for beginners and children *(www.upp.no)*.

3 Good mood guaranteed

Nordic reserve? Forget it! At least when it comes to fashion: *Moods of Norway* is all about flashy clothing collections *(Akersgata 18, Oslo,* photo). Eco-fashion with pop-colours and cool cuts can be found at Fin *(www.finoslo.com)*. The *Oslo Fashion Week* shows everything else that is hot in the fashion world twice a year. That is when the streets of the capital burst into colour *(www.oslofashionweek. com)*.

Shining example

4

Beaming hotels There is strong competition among hotels. That is why Norwegian hosts have thought up something special for holiday-makers. Old lighthouses have been turned into hotels in breathtaking surroundings. Storm-battered *Svinøy Lighthouse* on a deserted island nine sea miles from the coast is one of these destinations. You won't have to do without any comforts either; the service staff takes care of the lighthouse's guests and you arrive by helicopter *(Fosnavåg, www.62.no, photo right)*. *Molja Lighthouse* gives a warm welcome to ships shortly before they enter Ålesund Harbour. The interior of the 150-year-old building, which is also known as *Room 47*, is completely modern *(www.brosundet. no)*. *Hasugjegla Lighthouse* is more spacious. There is room for up to twelve guests in the 28 m (92 ft) high tower *(Smøla, www.fyropp levelser.no)*.

Water and snow

5

From the boat to the slopes Snow during the day and water at night. Winter sports-people use a ship 300 km (190 mi) north of the Arctic Circle as the stating point for their ski tours. There is a steady slope up what appears to be a never-ending mountain ridge. The spectacular view of the sea from the summit makes up for all your efforts – and then, there is the downhill run in powder snow! Lyngen Lodge specialises in this cool combination of a cruise and skiing *(Djupvik, Olderdalen, www.lyngen lodge.com)*.

IN A NUTSHELL

FISHING

Norwegian territorial waters are extremely productive with more than 200 species of fish, shellfish and crustaceans. Norway is still the world's largest fish exporter and the industry markets fish valued at 4.8 billion pounds (7.5 billion US$) yearly abroad (56 percent from farmed fish). The number of fishermen has sunk by around 80 percent since 1950 but the catch has remained almost constant. The threatened stocks of fish in the North Atlantic have lead the EU, Norway, Russia, Iceland, the Faroe Islands and Greenland to take measures against illegal fishing. One particularly controversial matter in foreign countries is whaling. Although it is permitted to shoot around 1000 minke whales, demand has declined to the extent that hardly any whaling now takes place.

LANGUAGES

There are two official languages in Norway: Bokmål and Nynorsk. The differences between the two are not very significant and are more of a linguistic-political nature. Nynorsk was created out of several dialects while Bokmål has its roots in Danish. Most books, magazines and newspapers are published in Bokmål. The people who live in a community decide which of the two languages will be used

Photo: Stave church in Hopperstad

A country with a high standard of living: Norway's young cultural scene and exemplary family policies set it apart

for teaching in primary schools. The pupils in secondary schools must have a written command of both languages.

MIDNIGHT SUN

The Arctic Circle runs through Nordland *fylke* at latitude 66°33' north; beyond this, the sun never sets around 23 June. The further north one goes, the longer it remains above the horizon.

Theoretically, the *midnattsol* can be seen from 13 May to 29 July at the North Cape; unfortunately, the view there is usually not ideal. In Tromsø, the sun does not set from 20 May to 22 July, and from 28 May to 14 July on the Lofoten Islands.

MILITARY

Norway's defence system consists of an army, air force and navy. It is compulsory for men between the ages of 18 and 44 to perform 12 months of military service; this is voluntary for women. Norway is NATO's north-eastern outpost. However, the common border with Russia also makes it necessary to have good relationships with the big neighbour to the east. Troops from other countries are only allowed to enter the country for manoeuvres and foreign weapons are not allowed on Norwegian territory.

MINERAL RESOURCES

Every year Norway invests more than 8.7 billion pounds (13.5 US$) in opening up new oil and gas fields on the Shelf. The most profitable deposits are in the Norwegian Sea and off the northern coast of the country. An industry with 30,000 immediate employees that produces more than one quarter of the gross domestic product relies on finding new fields. Environmental protection organisations recommend not developing all the fields to the north and west of the North Cape. They point out the extreme weather conditions and the effect of interfering with the delicate ecology of the Barents Sea. Mining has a long tradition in Norway but, with the exception of coal mining on Svalbard, it has lost its original importance. Today, only around 4,000 people work in Norwegian mines.

MUSIC

Norway was the home of Edvard Grieg (1843–1907) whose Peer Gynt Suite is one of the most often played pieces of classical music. The pianist Leif Ove Andsnes is one of the most prominent performers of classical music today. The cellist Truls Mørk and violinist Henning Kraggerud, who also likes to play jazz, are world-famous. Dag Arnesen is another pianist who surprised the international jazz world with his interpretations of

Norwegian folk music as did Tord Gustavsen and Helge Lien with their melodic but daring compositions for the same instrument. Silje Nergaard, with her haunting voice, also has her artistic roots in jazz but now sings ballads with a tendency towards pop music. The pop singers Maria Mena, Ingrid Olava and Marit Larsen also have fans outside of Norway. Bergen is considered the European capital of black metal – thanks to the group Immortal.

NATIONAL PARKS

There are 40 national parks on mainland Norway with a total area of almost 27,000 km² (10,425 mi²) and more than 80 other conservation areas are protected from exploitation. Altogether, 40,000 km² (15,444 mi²) are governed by countryside conservation legislation. This is intended to help preserve the varied fauna and flora and, at the same time, assure the rights of the individual to be able to move freely in the natural environment. Details of the Norway's national parks can be found under *www.visitnorway. com/en/Articles/Theme/What-to-do/ Attractions/Nature/National-parks*.

NORTHERN LIGHTS

Fascinating and full of surprises – the northern lights (aurora borealis) is the epitome of nature's aesthetics. It is caused by electrons that come into contact with the Earth's magnetic field in great numbers and at high speed and collide with the upper layers of the atmosphere where various kinds of gas glow in different colours. The northern lights can be observed frequently on cold, clear winter evenings north of the Arctic Circle. When you see it for the first time, you will immediately forget the physics: drifting, green veils of mist fill up the skies, light-blue arches dart over the horizon and, between all this, a multi-coloured shower of light falls onto the snowy landscape, a mountain lake or the sea. You will just look for a tree to lean against or a rock to sit on and let yourself be mesmerised by the beauty.

POLAR HISTORY

No other country is as proud of its polar history as Norway. All Norwegians know about the expeditions undertaken by their countrymen by ship or on skis, alone or in groups, to the most distant

Pole by air in his airship, *Norge*. In 1990, Erling Kagge and Børge Ousland made it to the North Pole without any outside assistance. Kagge skied to the South Pole in 1992/93 and Ousland reached the North Pole alone in 1994. Ousland, who has been to the North Pole four times and climbed Mount Everest as well, was also on board the fibreglass trimaran Northern Passage that was the first to sail around the entire North Pole in 2010.

Celestial cinema in Kautokeino: the Northern Lights, a spectacular natural phenomenon

corners of the globe. The pioneer was Fridjtof Nansen who set out on a three-year expedition to the North Arctic Ocean on his ship the *Fram* in 1893. Together with his companion Hjalmar Johansen, he also attempted to reach the North Pole on skis and with dog sleds. In 1911, Roald Amundsen was the first to reach the South Pole. He traversed the North-west and North-east Passages and, in 1926, was the first person to reach the North

POLITICS

Norway is Social-Democratic through and through. The highly-developed social state with a large percentage of government employees can be financed as long as the oil fund keeps on growing at such a dizzying rate. The state administers the oil and gas reserves and holds 67 percent of the shares in the Statoil international petrol conglomerate. Although the 167 representatives in parliament *(Storting)* come from seven different parties, every-day political life is rather uneventful. However, pressure to decrease taxes increases with every election campaign and the right-wing Progress Party dreams of Norway as the 'Kuwait of the North' without any taxes at all and little work. The representatives and ministers do their job and get paid – this is calculated according to professional experience and age, and can be viewed by anyone interested. In this way, politicians remain 'people like you and me'.

RELIGION

Laws, songs and monuments show that Christianity had gained a foothold in Norway by the middle of the 11th century. The first dioceses were established shortly before 1100; Nidaros (later, Trondheim) became a bishop's seat in 1152. In 1537, the Reformation was ordered by royal decree from Copenhagen. From the early 17th century, Luther's teachings became the sole religion in Norway. Today, around 86 percent of Norwegians are Protestant and members of the State Church; approximately 380,000 belong to other religions – mainly the Pentecostal Church and Islam. Barely 46,000 are members of the Catholic Church.

ROYAL FAMILY

Harald V has been Norway's king since 1991. As was the case with Harald, his son Haakon also married a commoner, but this has never really bothered the Norwegians or played a significant role. Royalists and republicans alike find it important that the king is something special but also 'one of us'. The career chosen by Princess Märtha Louise, Haakon's younger sister, has taken her in a different direction which is why she appears in the weeklies more often than her parents or brother. After studying physiotherapy and literature, she has devoted herself to writing and

giving readings of fairy tales and other stories as well as founding a centre for alternative methods of treatment.

SAMI

A conservative estimation shows that around 70,000 people belong to the Sami people, Scandinavia's native population. Forty to forty-five thousand of them live in Norway – approximately 25,000 in the Finnmark *fylke*. Since around 1980, efforts have been made to improve their legal situation in Norway and the Sami parliament *Sameting* was officially opened in Karasjok in 1989. This has played in major role in establishing the Sami people's renewed self-assuredness. They once again celebrate their national holiday on 6 February and have been successful in asserting their rights to administer a large section of the Finnmark government district. In the central regions of Samiland, Sami – one of the Finno-Ugric languages – is in everyday use and is even the second official language in some communities. Along with reindeer farming and fishing, general farming, crafts and the service sector are the most important sources of income for the Sami.

STAVE CHURCHES

Traditional stave churches are simple, comparatively small, wooden buildings with narrow naves and walls constructed of posts. The oldest of the 29 stave churches that have been preserved was built in the 12th century. The reason that it has remained standing for so long is its sturdy foundation. It is made up of posts and planks placed on joists that prevent them from decaying. The central decorative elements are the carved ornaments in the entrance area. This traditional ornamentation can probably be traced back to the Viking's animal decorations. Heddal Stavkirke in the Telemark region and Borgund

Stavkirke near Lærdal on Sognefjord are two classic examples of stave churches and very popular with visitors.

THEATRE

Plays by Henrik Ibsen (1828–1906) are performed in theatres all over the world. Figures such as Nora, Peer Gynt, John Gabriel Borkman and The Lady from the Sea have been portrayed in all major languages. Ibsen was a controversial figure in his native country while he was still alive but now Skien, his home town, has an annual culture festival to celebrate the poet and playwright. A similar event is held every second year in the National Theatre in Oslo. And, there are other Norwegian playwrights of international renown, too. In the mid-1990s, plays by Jon Fosse started to be performed in other European countries. *The Name*, *Night Sings its Song*, *The Child*, *A Summer's Day* and *Sleep* have even been frequently staged in theatres in Asia and America.

THE FAMILY

Equality between the sexes has already been largely achieved and legal differences between marital and non-marital partnerships almost completely eliminated. In most families, both parents work. Norway has the third highest birth rate in Europe and Norwegian women have an average 1.98 children. The social security for both mother and father is exemplary. Parents are able to divide the 47 weeks of maternity leave at full pay (or 57 weeks at 80 percent) as they choose, and one of the parents can stay at home with the baby for at least two years without losing his or her job.

TROLLS

You should believe in them simply because there are so many of them in Norwegian fairy tales and legends – and

souvenir shops. Trolls live deep in the woods and are very difficult to find. Depending on what kind they are, they either live in

The traditional Sami dress is rarely seen today

families or are terrifying loners. They look like gnarled trees, have enormous noses and straggly fur, smell to high heaven and only come out of their caves at night. They are not particularly threatening because they want to have as little to do with people as possible and it is easy to trick them. So, on your ramblings through the woods of Norway, keep your eyes peeled but don't be too afraid.

FOOD & DRINK

The favourite meal of Norwegians who respect tradition is called *mors kjøttkaker* – mother's meatballs – which are a perfect illustration of Norwegian cuisine: simple and nourishing, and pepper and salt are the only things you might need to add.

In general, more fish dishes than meat ones are served in Norway and simple preparation is the name of the game. For example, after it has soaked in hot water for fifteen minutes, salted cod is served with carrots, potatoes and melted butter – and that's all. Other fish dishes include *fiskekaker* (fish cakes), *fiskeboller* (fish balls) and *fiskepudding*. They can be bought in

any supermarket and are prepared with a white sauce or simply warmed up in the oven.

It is amazing to see how many dishes from fishing and farming societies have made their way into the Norwegian kitchen. Pancakes and milk pudding are a fine choice on Saturday and roasts, boiled fish or just meatballs are served on Sunday. Mutton *(fårekjøtt)* is normally only prepared in the slaughtering season in autumn; a popular stew is white cabbage with mutton *(fårikål)*.

Insider's consider two fish dishes from the Middle Ages a delicatessen, but not everybody agrees with this. *Lutefisk* is dried cod

Fiskeboller and *finnebiff*: fish plays a major role in Norwegian cooking but there are also many tasty meat dishes

soaked in brine that is served at Christmas with boiled potatoes, fried bacon and puréed peas. Especially in East Norway, fish fans look forward to *rakørret*: a thoroughly cleaned trout is soaked in brine for a few weeks and then eaten with onions, cream and potato pancakes. This really stinks while it is fermenting but even the most sceptical will change their minds when they taste it.

The tradition of eating a sheep's head in West Norway is definitely not merely a question of taste. It is only possible to overcome one's initial aversion to eating flaps of chin, sheeps' ears and eyes with plenty of beer and aquavit. Fans consider eyes a real speciality but, to be honest, many only try it once!

Finnebiff: thin slices of reindeer meat that used to be scraped off the bones and

LOCAL SPECIALITIES

▶ **Eplekake med is** – warm apple cake with ice-cream
▶ **Fiskekaker** – Fishcakes; East Norwegian variety: salted whitefish fillets with potato flour and onions mixed into a dough that is then formed into cakes and fried
▶ **Klippfisk** – Dried cod, boiled and served with boiled potatoes, carrots, melted butter and parsley
▶ **Kokt torsk** – Boiled cod, accompanied by carrots, boiled potatoes and melted butter
▶ **Lammesteik** – Roast lamb – a classic in autumn – seasoned with thyme, rosemary and garlic
▶ **Lefse** – Flat pancakes made of sour cream, syrup, sugar, baking powder and wheat flour, served with sugar and butter
▶ **Moltekrem** – Whipped cream mixed with jam
▶ **Ovnsbakt laks** – Salmon, stuffed with leek, celeriac and cabbage, baked in the oven and seasoned with salt and garlic pepper

▶ **Ovnsbakt steinbit** – Wolffish fillets baked in the oven, served with onions, apples and mushrooms fried in butter with apple juice and thyme
▶ **Pasta med røkt laks** – Pasta with a sauce of onions and fish bouillon, cream and strips of (smoked) salmon or trout
▶ **Raspeballer** – Potato dumplings with barley flour and diced bacon, served with puréed swedes and boiled potatoes. Accompanied by mutton or smoked sausage. In East Norway, this dish is called *komle*
▶ **Røkt elgsteik** – Smoked elk meat, braised in the oven (photo, left) with root vegetables, Brussels sprouts, game sauce and boiled potatoes
▶ **Rømmegrøt** – Purée of sour cream, wheat flour or semolina and salt, refined with sugar and cinnamon. Salted meat is served as a side dish (photo, right).
▶ **Trollkrem** – Cranberries mixed with whipped cream, served cold

buried in snow was originally a Sami dish and is an example of their close harmony living with the gifts of nature. It is seared while it is still frozen and stewed before the sauce is finished with a good portion of sour cream. Only salt and pepper are added to the meat before it is served with boiled potatoes and fresh cranberries. Besides reindeer meat, deer and elk are becoming increasingly popular – mos probably because there are an increasing number of wild animals and hunters and the Norwegians are prepared to spend more for their Sunday roast.

In spite of a well-developed feeling for tradition in Norway, international convenience foods are now playing a more important role in the country. Pizza and roast chicken have become part of a Saturday evening in watching television and, if in a hurry, even adults resort to *pølse med brød*, hotdogs, that can be bought at any garage and all *gatekjøkken* (snack bars).

On the other hand, there are severe restrictions on the purchase of alcoholic beverages. Wine and spirits are only available in shops run by the *Vinmonopolet* and there are only around 260 of these in the whole of Norway – most are self-service shops in the major cities. The selection ranges from strong ale, wine from all corners of the world to spirits – but these must not have an alcohol content above 60 percent. Beer with a low alcohol content can be bought almost everywhere in supermarkets. If statistics can be believed, Norway's alcohol policies have been successful: while the average consumption in the EU is around 11 litres per year, it is less than 7 litres in Norway. However, continental drinking habits are starting to make themselves felt and this has led to *mors kjøttkaker* occasionally being accompanied by a glass of red wine – and, in general, alcohol consumption is rising. There are still some individual hotels that, for ideological reasons, have not applied for a licence to sell alcohol. If you go to have a meal in a good city restaurant, you will not notice any restrictions or voluntary abstention from alcohol but you might be a bit hesitant when you see the prices. The high taxation on alcohol means that a bottle of wine will cost more than a tasty plate of game (around 315 NOK). Better

A snack in the open air in Nusfjord on the Lofoten

restaurants charge around 63 NOK for half a litre of beer. This means that the best decision might be to enjoy your meal in its pristine state without any alcohol and order a carafe of ice-cold tap water.

SHOPPING

Nobody travels to Norway just to go shopping. However, the high food prices do not necessarily apply to other articles and if you buy products 'Made in Norway' they will give you years of pleasure. Articles made of wood and knitwear, for example, have an important feature in common: natural materials and solid workmanship. The best selection of typical Norwegian souvenirs can be found in the *Husfliden shops (www.husfliden.no)* in all major cities where expertly-trained staff will help you find just what you are looking for.

FASHION

Look out for the *tilbud* (bargain) signs when strolling around the larger towns in summer. The branches of international chains attract customers with their special offers that stand comparison with prices at home. There are even Norwegian-made jeans and the products of Norway's trendsetting *Moods of Norway* company *(www.moodsofnorway.com)* can be purchased in many cities – the collection has even crossed the Atlantic and reached the USA.

KNITWEAR

Scarves, mittens, woollen socks, cardigans and headgear with traditional Norwegian patterns make long-lasting, attractive souvenirs. Woollen underwear and socks from Norway are warm, functional and pleasant to wear. The 😊 INSIDER TIP *Janus (www.janus.no)* knitted-goods company's collection includes many organic products made of pure wool that are perfect for hiking or wearing in winter and are extremely cosy. If they are hand-knit and made of local wool, Norwegian pullovers are expensive but also of the very best quality. It is important to ask who produced them because the patterns used by Asian manufactures are almost identical with those made in Norway. The *Dale of Norway (dale.no)* label has been successful in combining traditional and modern design.

SMOKED SALMON & CAVIAR

You can recognise good smoked salmon by its darker colour; it is dryer and smells more strongly of smoke than lower-quality fish. Generally speaking, less salt means

Plain, well-made and relatively expensive:
if you are interested in quality, you will find
what you're looking for in Norway

more taste. Try the salmon before you buy it. Shrink-wrapped salmon from the supermarket can also be good quality. A simple alternative is dried cod *(tørrfisk)* that can be bought in any supermarket that you can transform into a delicious *bacalhau* when you get home. Or, take a stock of tubes of caviar with you. This spread made of cod roe is healthy, non-perishable – and not even very expensive.

SPORTS GEAR

Anybody who has hiked in a Norwegian fjell knows what equipment is needed. Everything must be of the highest quality – from absolutely dependable hiking boots to the cap on your head. *Bergans (www. bergans.de)* is a 'thoroughly Norwegian' producer which mainly specialises in premium rucksacks and tents. *Helly Hansen (www.hellyhansen.com)* has a smaller range of products that will satisfy even the most demanding – but at a higher price. Formerly a producer of clothing for sailing and skiing, today, the Oslo enterprise focuses on winter sports. The articles of these two firms are available in any good sportswear shop.

WOODEN GOODS & CHEESE SLICERS

Wooden mugs, serving plates and bowls make popular presents as do knives. Produced on a small scale mainly in the countryside, such items demonstrate how natural materials have their individual aesthetics and are long lasting. One of the oldest Norwegian inventions is the cheese slicer that is available either in stainless steel or in silver and is often beautifully decorated. A must for any 'Norwegian night' you have after you return home.

THE PERFECT ROUTE

THE CAPITAL FROM ABOVE

① *Oslo* → p. 41 is where you tour begins, but don't forget to visit the Opera House or Holmenkollen ski jump before you leave. These two world-famous sites are more than enough reason to plan some time before setting out on your trip.

VALLEYS, TRADITIONS AND THE OPEN FJELL

After leaving Oslo, head west: turn off the E16 onto the Rv7 road near Hønefoss. You will come across fewer and fewer settlements and more and more woods, lakes and ranges of hills will come into view. Even before you reach the watershed in Hallingdal Valley, you will notice small wooden houses and farms, raging rivers and scattered villages that have developed out of former farmsteads. Now, the route takes you up to Europe's most extensive plateau, the **②** *Hardangervidda* → p. 57, where you will have your first opportunity to try out those new hiking boots you brought with you.

WALLS OF ROCK, FRUIT & PLENTY OF CULTURE

The Norway of the fjords begins in the small town of Eidfjord. The roads wind past steep rock faces, the blue and green of the water of the inlets, majestic waterfalls and verdant meadows. The **③** *Hardanger* → p. 56 region is the birthplace of national romanticism and the country's main fruit growing area. Further on in **④** *Bergen* → p. 52, you will discover a pulsating cultural city that is also the heart of a diversified holiday region.

DEEP DOWN IN THE FJORDS

⑤ *Sognefjord* → p. 59, **⑥** *Nordfjord* → p. 61 (photo, top) and Storfjord – the North Sea flows deep into the interior of the country. Here, you will have no choice but to adjust your tempo to the topography – slow down and enjoy the unforgettable breaks: the ferry trip from Hellesylt (Road 60) into the **⑦** *Geirangerfjord* → p. 51, a stroll through the Art Nouveau town of **⑧** *Ålesund* → p. 48, a detour to the fishing village **⑨** *Bud* → p. 59 and to the **⑩** *Atlantic Ocean Route* → p. 59 (Road 664).

CATHEDRAL CITY IN THE HEART OF THE COUNTRY

The fjord district ends a little to the east of Kristiansund. The forests become thicker as you travel furher inland – until you catch sight of yet another fjord shortly before **⑪** *Trondheim* → p. 67. You will experience a fascinating mix of a wealth of

Experience the diversity of Norway on a trip over several days to cathedrals and magical fjords

history and a modern university town in this cathedral city.

UNBELIEVABLE COASTAL SCENERY

Your ⑫ *Hurtigruten* → p. 75 adventure begins after your night in Trondheim. The ship glides tranquilly up the coast of the Helgeland district to the north, crosses the Arctic Circle, and drops anchor in ⑬ *Bodø* → p. 72 sixteen hours later (photo, right).

LOFOTEN WONDERLAND

Bodø is the gateway to the ⑭ *Lofoten* → p. 80. Do you still have some time? Then stay on board and travel on through dreamlike ⑮ *Trollfjord* → p. 84 and only turn around in the harbour town of Stokmarknes. It is shortly after midnight and it is still as bright as day. In the afternoon, you set off to the south; into Trolllfjord again and then on to Bodø. Night has fallen, you meet the pub crawlers who just don't want to go to bed in this town; there will be plenty of time to sleep on the train back to Trondheim.

SELDOM SEEN ANIMALS, TOWERING MOUNTAINS & SKI ARENAS

You drive to the south: over the pass in the ⑯ *Dovrefjell Mountains* → p. 64 where Europe's largest herd of musk oxen roams and close to the gigantic mountains in the ⑰ *Rondane* → p. 40 national park – two boundless hiking areas with many mountain peaks over

3100 km (1900 mi). Driving time: 65 hours. Detailed map of the route on the back cover, in the road atlas and the pull-out map

2000 m (6600 ft) high. In the Gudbrandsalen Valley, the landscape widens towards the Olympic city of ⑱ *Lillehammer* → p. 39. Take some time to visit the winter-sport arenas and Maihaugen open-air museum – unadulterated Norway again!

THE SOUTH

Emerging from cool mountain lakes, raging rivers force their way through dense forests. Bays lie hidden along the coast with its countless skerries, shiny washed boulders and ports that have preserved the charm of the steamship age.

Swimming in water that is above 20°C (68°F) warm is just one of the many attractions of a summer holiday in Sørlandet, the coastal strip along the Skagerrak. There are plenty of beaches with shallow water and moorings but the really peaceful places are far from the coast road.

Although South Norway is a destination for water sports enthusiasts, it is also popular with hikers where, in spite of only being sparsely covered with vegetation, the fjell – the long expanse of high hills – provides a foretaste of the amazingly rich arctic fauna and flora. The south of Norway is full of rich colour, a great variety of landscapes and is not at all cold.

FREDRIKSTAD

(133 E5) (⨍ D17) **The Fredriksten fortress was erected in 1663, captured by Swedish troops in 1814, and given up as a military base in 1903.**

With its paved streets and Empire-style houses, this city and fortress in the ex-

Urban Norway and the wilderness beyond: charming places and verdant nature hidden between islands and skerries

treme south-east of the country is now both a cultural monument and tourist destination. Norway's longest river, the Glomma, also flows into the Oslofjord here and this has led to many industries, both small and large, being established on its banks. The harbour is one of the largest in the south of Norway. With a population of some 72,000, Fredrikstad is the largest city and capital of the Østfold *fylke*.

FREDRIKSTADE DOMKIRKE

The cathedral was built in 1880 and restored in 1954. The stained-glass windows by Emanuel Vigeland (1875–1948) – the younger brother of the better-know sculptor Gustav Vigeland – are well-worth seeing and the organ is a delight. *Tue–Thu 11am–2pm, Fri 11am–1pm*

ISEGRAN FORT AND KONGSTEN FORT
Two outer sections of the fortress have been preserved: Isegran is an archaeological station run by the University of Oslo; Kongsten, mainly an idyllic place to lie down and take a rest on warm summer days.

FOOD & DRINK

INSIDER TIP ▶ GAFFEL & KARAFFEL
A fascinating combination of traditional Norwegian lunch dishes and delicious sushi. *Stortorvet | tel. 69 31 03 60 | Moderate*

JACOB AALL BRASSERIE OG BAR
When the weather is fine in summer this restaurant is the ideal spot for a quick meal or cool glass of beer. *Storgata 15 | tel. 69 31 11 00 | www.jacobaall.no | Budget*

SHOPPING

GLASHYTTA
The products made by the Kenyan glass artist Abel Sawe are characterised by their strong colours and unusual forms. There is a small museum and shop. *Tornesveien 1 | Gamlebyen | www.glashytta-gamlebyen.no*

WHERE TO STAY

HANKØ FJORDHOTELL & SPA
Here, pure relaxation is top priority. Swimming pool, tennis court, fitness room and a spacious spa area, surrounded by magnificent countryside with forests on the banks of the fjord where you can go for a stroll. *192 rooms | Hankø | tel. 69 38 28 50 | www.hankohotell.no | Expensive*

INFORMATION
Turistkontor | Torvgaten 59A | tel. 69 30 46 00 | www.fredrikstad-hvaler.no

You can almost touch them: the peaks in the Jotunheimen alpine region

GARNLEBYEN (FORTRESS AND OLD CITY)
The peaceful old-city quarter with its cobblestone streets is surrounded by a moat, grass-covered ramparts, bastions and city gates. This is the location of numerous galleries, arts and crafts shops, studios and restaurants. The *turistkontor* organises tours through the old city. *www.festningsbyen.no*

WHERE TO GO

HVALER (133 E5) (*D17*)

Sailors and sun worshipers love the Hvaler Islands; they can be reached by driving over bridges and through a tunnel on Road 108. The most beautiful is the southern-most island INSIDER TIP *Kirkeøy*. Beaches and the sea stretch in all directions as far as the eye can see. The *Hvaler Kirke (15 June–15 Aug, daily 9am–3pm)*, dating from before 1100, is located in the main town *Skjærhalden* (25 km/15½mi south of Fredrikstad). *www.fredrikstad-hvaler.no*

JOTUN-HEIMEN

(132 C1–2) (*C14*) **Translated literally, Jotunheimen means 'homeland of the giants'. It is Norway's only high mountain range and has been a popular destination for hikers, mountaineers and skiers since time immemorial.**

Here, a chain of mountains over 2000 m (6600 ft) high stretches out one after the other, some of them crowned with glaciers. However, even the highest of them, Galdhøpiggen – at 2469 m (8100 ft) the highest mountain in Norway and all of Scandinavia – can be climbed by children.

SIGHTSEEING

INSIDER TIP KLIMAPARK 2469 ☺

The world's first climate park has been established in northern Jotunheimen. Visitors can experience how the climate has changed over the past 2000 years in an ice tunnel beneath Galdhøpiggen Mountain: 300–440 m of permafrost, glacial ice and finds discovered as a result of the latest ice melt. *Daily excursions end of July–end of August, Thu–Sun, start 10am in the Juvasshytta mountain hut | tickets 300 NOK at the hut or from the tourist information office in Lom | www.oppland. no/klimapark2469*

NORSK FJELLMUSEUM ●

The museum in Lom provides a historical overview of how man has made use of the mountains and the effects climate and nature have had on Norwegian culture. *May–mid-June and mid-Aug–Sept Mon–Fri 9am–4pm, Sat, Sun 11am–5pm, mid-June–mid-Aug, Mon–Fri 9am–7pm, Sat, Sun 10am–7pm | entrance fee 50 NOK | www. fjell.museum.no*

SOGNEFJELLSVEI

Road 55 from Lom in the north-east to Skjolden in the south-west has been

---

MARCO POLO HIGHLIGHTS

★ **Risør**
Pure South-Norwegian idyll in a maritime setting → p. 39

★ **Olympia Park**
Even an experience for those not interested in sports: the Lillehammer complex → p. 39

★ **Holmenkollen**
The view of Oslo from the ski jump is incomparable → p. 42

★ **Nasjonalgalleriet**
In Oslo: the finest collection of Norwegian painting → p. 43

★ **Operahuset**
Norway's new landmark – in Oslo, directly on the fjord → p. 44

★ **Heddal Stavkirke**
The most impressive of the stave churches still standing → p. 46

established for tourists as a 'green road' and runs through icy heights. With a place to stop for a rest at 1400 m (4600 ft), glacier snouts, hiking trails and places to fish to the left and right of the road the journey is an eventful encounter with the Norwegian mountain world. *www.turistveg.no*

FOOD & DRINK

INSIDER TIP ▶ BAKERIET I LOM

A Norwegian master chef studied all the finer points of the baker's art and opened a bakery and café at the Prestefosse waterfall in Lom – a joy for all the senses. *www.bakerietilom.no*

SPORTS & ACTIVITIES

GALDHØPIGGEN ⚜

Norway's highest toll road (turn off Road 55 near Galdesand) leads to *Juvasshytta* (1840 m/6000 ft), a hut run by the Norwegian Hiking Association DNT. This is where the climb to the summit of

Norway's highest mountain Galdhøpiggen (2469 m/8100 ft) begins. In summer, there are guided tours over a glacier to the top at 10am; the way up and down takes a total of five hours.

WHERE TO STAY

JOTUNHEIMEN FJELLSTUE

A classic fjell guesthouse: simple, rustic but cosy, amid the amazing mountain scenery and with many possibilities for outdoor activities. *18 rooms | on Road 55 | tel. 61 21 29 18 | www.jotunheimen-fjellstue.no | Moderate*

STORHAUGEN GÅRD ⚜

This farm is situated at an altitude of 800 m (2600 ft) with a view of mountain peaks soaring to a height of more than 2000 m (6600 ft). Flats in the main house or in the neighbouring cabins; everything is simple but well cared-for. You can even help out on the farm. The goats follow guests into the mountains. E-mail reservations preferred. *70 beds | near Galdesand on Road 55 | tel. 61 21 20 69 | www.storhaugengard.no | info@storhaugen gard.no | Budget–Moderate*

INFORMATION

Turistinformasjon | in the Norsk Fjellmuseum in Lom | tel. 61 21 29 90 | www. visitjotunheimen.com

KRISTIAN-SAND

(132 C6) (*ฌ B18*) **The harbour city (population: 68,000) sees itself as the heart of the 'Riviera of the North'.**
The weather is stable and the wonderful skerry garden on the Skagerrak offers

magnificent recreational facilities for families, sun worshippers and water sports enthusiasts. The right-angled layout of the streets was ordered by the Danish-Norwegian King Christian IV who established the town on a sandy promontory in 1641.

can also visit workshops, small shops, a tobacco mill and an underground hut that was used by Norwegian partisans in World War II. *In summer Tue–Fri 10am–5pm, Sat–Mon noon–5pm | entrance fee 50 NOK | a little to the east of the town | www. vestagdermuseet.no*

Summer in Sørlandet: picturesque residential area on the harbour in Kristiansand

SIGHTSEEING

MØVIK FORT
This fortress 8 km (5 mi) to the west of the city was constructed in 1942 by the German occupation forces and has a wonderful view over the Skagerrak. The most interesting exhibit in the battery emplacement is an almost 20-metre-long canon. *May–mid-June and mid-Aug–Sept Mon–Wed 11am–3pm, Thu–Sun 11am–45pm, mid-June–mid-Aug daily 11am–6pm | entrance fee 65 NOK | Road 456 towards Vågsbygd | www.nasjonalefestningsverk.no*

VEGT-AGDER-MUSEET
Open-air museum with a Setesdal farm complex of ten buildings – one of them with a living room from the 17th century – and townhouses from Kristiansand. You

SHOPPING

Kvadraturen, especially on warm summer days, the right-angled layout of the town centre is an ideal place to take a relaxed stroll. There are many small shops, cafés and restaurants in the two pedestrian precincts *Markensgata* and *Rådhusgata*.

BEACHES

(132 C6) (*ဩ B–C18*) The typical places for taking a swim are small oases of sand between the grey boulders on the shore. You will find large sandy beaches in *Bertnes Bay* (3 km/1¾mi east of Kristiansand) and *Hamresanden* (11 km/6¾mi east). These, along with *Bystranda* in Kristiansand itself and *Skotteviga* near Lillesand (31 km/19¼mi to the east), are

A game of beach volleyball on the beach at Mandal, the most southerly town in Norway

among the cleanest beaches in South Norway.

WHERE TO STAY

BELLEVUE VILLA
Anyone looking for a room or small flat with a view of the Skagerrak for their stay in Kristiansand will be able to sleep comfortably here and go easy on their holiday budget. The furnishings are fairly simple. Breakfast is not included but, with the help of the coffee machine, microwave and refrigerator in the rooms, you will be able to take care of this for yourself. *6 rooms, 2 flats | Kirkegata 2D | tel. 45 80 68 86 and 45 80 58 85 | www.bellevuevilla.no | Budget–Moderate*

INSIDER TIP YESS! HOTEL
Good things come in small packages – for families and young people. A perfect location between the centre of town and the ferry port; very small rooms (but good mattresses!); the evening and breakfast buffets are full of surprises – sometimes homemade pizza, sometimes tapas. *55 rooms | Tordenskjoldsgate 12 | tel. 38 70 15 70 | www.yesshotel.no | Budget*

INFORMATION

Kristiansand Turistkontor | Rådhusgate 6 | Tel. 38 12 13 14 | www.sorlandet.com

WHERE TO GO

CAPE LINDESNES ☀ (132 B6) (⨌ B18)
The lighthouse on Norway's South Cape, built in 1915, stands on a small hill 80 km (50 mi) to the west of Kristiansand. The *Lighthouse Museum (in summer daily 10am–8pm, at other times 11am–5pm | entrance fee 50 NOK | www.lindesnesfyr. no)*, built by blasting away the rock, is well worth a visit.

MANDAL (132 C6) (⨌ B18)
This once important seafaring town (pop. 10,500) with pretty wooden houses

in its centre, lies at the mouth of the River Mandalselva. If the weather is fine in summer, you should postpone your stroll until the evening and go to one of the many city beaches during the day for a swim. Today, wool is once again washed, woven and spun in the woollen factory *Sjølingstad Uldvarefabrik* that was opened in 1894 *(in summer daily 11am–5pm, tours at 11am, 1 and 3pm | entrance free, tours 50 NOK | around 6 km (3¾mi) to the west of Mandal, turn off the E 39 | www.vestag dermuseet.no/sjolingstad)*. Visitors to this lively museum can take an active part and see how Norwegian wool eventually turns into a piece of clothing. *Mandal is 41 km (25½mi) to the west of Kristiansand | www. regionmandal.com*

RISØR ★ (133 D5) *(ØØ C17–18)*

The 'white town on the Skaggerak' (pop. 4500) with wonderful areas of wooden houses and impressive patrician residences along the harbour promenade is the most important gathering place for all Norwegian wooden-boat fans (festival beginning of August). The *Hellige Aands Kirke (Holy Spirit Church | tours in summer Mon–Fri noon–2pm)* was built in 1647 and is Norway's oldest Baroque church. *Moen Camping (tel. 37 15 50 91 | www.moen camping.no)*, with cabins and flats, camping site and beach, is only 10 km (6¼mi) from the centre of town. *116 km (72 mi) north-east of Kristiansand | www.risor.no*

LILLE- HAMMER

(133 E2) *(ØØ D15)* **The small town with a population of 20,000 on the northern tip of Mjøsa Lake, Norway's largest inland lake, is the gateway to Gudbrandsdalen Valley.**

The 1994 Winter Olympic Games were held in Lillehammer. Some of the sports complexes can be used by visitors. The Lysgård-bakkane ski jump literally springs into view and, from the top, you can get an impression of what a jumper feels just before he zooms off down the slope.

SIGHTSEEING

MAIHAUGEN

More than 170 buildings will not only give you an idea of the rural culture of Gudbrandsdalen but also of craftsmanship from all over Norway. Many of the workshops are still in use. Changing exhibitions. *June–Aug daily 10am–5pm, shorter opening hours at other times | entrance fee 140 NOK | www.maihaugen.no*

NORGES OLYMPISKE MUSEUM

The 1994 Winter Games (including a multimedia show) form the core of the exhibition in the Håkonshalle and there is also a section dealing with Olympic history. *June–Aug daily 10am–5pm, at other times Tue–Sun 11am–4pm | entrance fee 80 NOK | www.maihaugen.no*

OLYMPIA PARK ★ ☀

With a ski jump (simulator), freestyle arena, ski stadium and bob and toboggan runs, on which you can travel downhill at speeds of up to 100 kph (62 mph) in a four-man bike-bob in summer. *June–Aug Sat 11am–6pm, Sun 11am–4pm | Bike-bob 220 NOK | www.olympiaparken.no*

FOOD & DRINK

BLÅMANN RESTAURANT & BAR

First-class lunch dishes from north, south, west and east in the centre of town. 'Hunter's Soup' is especially recommendable. *Lilletorvet 1| tel. 61 26 22 03 | www. blaamann.com | Moderate*

BIRKEBEINEREN HOTEL & APARTMENTS
On a slope between the ski jump and the city, the atmosphere is somewhere between that of a hotel and fjell guesthouse. A great deal of wood and cosiness and excellent service. A place for family stays in winter and summer. *48 rooms, 40 apartments | Birkebeinervegen 24 | tel. 61 05 00 80 | www.birkebeineren.no | Moderate*

LILLEHAMMER VANDRERHJERN STASJONEN
As simple as a youth hostel but all rooms have showers and WC. Towels and breakfast are included in the price. *29 rooms (80 beds) | Jernbarnetorget 2 | in train station | tel. 61 26 00 24 | www.815 mjosa. no | Budget*

Turistkontor | Jernbarnetoget 2 | tel. 61 28 98 00 | www.lillehammer.com

HAMAR (133 E2) *(𝄞 D15)*
This town (pop. 28,200) 60 km (37¼mi) to the south-east was the spiritual centre of Norway from the Christianisation of the country to the Reformation in 1537. The INSIDER TIP *ruins of the cathedral*, preserved under a fascinating glass pyramid, and the partially excavated *bishop's palace* from the 13th century are part of ● *Hedmarksmuseet* open-air museum located picturesquely on the banks of the Mjøsa *(23 May–mid-June and mid-Aug–early Sept Tue–Sun 10am–4pm, mid-June–mid-Aug daily 10am–5pm | free entrance to grounds, 80 NOK for entrance to buildings | Strandveien 100 | www.hedmarksmuseet. no)*. In the *Norwegian Railway Museum (July–15 Aug daily 10am–5pm, other times*

Tue–Sun 11am–3pm | entrance fee 75 NOK | Strandveien 163 | www.norskjernbane museum.no) you will not only see steam locomotives but also Norway's first train station that has been reconstructed here.

PEER-GYNT-VEIEN ⛷
(133 D1–2) *(𝄞 C–D 14–15)*
The 66 km (41 mi)-long toll road branches off Road 254 near Svingvoll. There are many lookout spots at heights of more than 1000 m (3300 ft) from where you will have a magnificent view of the Jotun heimen, Rondane and Dovrefjell Mountains. Both sides of the road are lined with guesthouses and log-cabins in the traditional style but people mainly come here for the countryside in which they can go hiking and fishing, watch elks, play golf or go cycling. The ● INSIDER TIP *Peer Gynt Festival* is held every year near *Vinstra* at the northern end of the road *(entrance fee approx. 600 NOK | www.peergynt.no)*: Henrik Ibsen's – and Norway's – most famous play is performed against the absolutely beautiful scenery of Lake Gålåvanet accompanied by the incidental music composed by Edvard Grief. *Four toll stations (60 NOK each) | www.peergyntvegen.no*

RONDANE NATIONAL PARK ⛷
(133 D1) *(𝄞 C–D14)*
The national park between the Gudbrands dalen and Østerdalen valleys is part of a mountain range – almost one fifth of its total area is classified as an alpine region. You will easily recognise traces of the last Ice Age in the ravines, gigantic terraces and depressions. Rodane is a perfect hiking area for young and old and it is comparatively easy to climb some of the 2000 m (6600 ft) high peaks. The *Rondane Spa Høyfjellshotell og Hytter (60 rooms | in Mysuseter, turn off the E6 near Odda | tel. 61 20 90 90 | www.rondane.no | Budget)* is a fine place to unwind with cross-country

skiing in winter, hiking through the endless expanse of the Rodane Mountains in summer, and a complete spa package in the evening: massage, treatments, yoga and swimming before having a delicious meal and relaxing in front of the fireplace. *www.nasjonalparkriket.no*

of Oslo near Akershus Fortress. The 'citizen's quarter' near Frognerparken and the multicultural Grønland suburb to the east of the main station are also well worth seeing. Oslo's smart shopping street Karl Johans gate stretches from the railway station to the Royal Palace; un-

Brick eye-catcher: Stortinget, the parliament building on Karl Johans gate in Oslo

OSLO

MAP INSIDE BACK COVER
(133 E4) *(∭ D16)* **The small capital city with a vast hinterland: Norway's metropolis (pop. 575,000) at the foot of the Oslofjord climbs up the slopes of the wooded Nordmarka.**

Oslo first became the seat of the Norwegian royal family under King Håkon V (1299–1319). The town was called Christiania from the 14th to the beginning of the 19th century when still part of Denmark and overshadowed by Copenhagen, Bergen and Trondheim. It only started to flourish again at the end of the 19th century and in 1925 it was given its old name once more. You definitely should visit the historic district

fortunately, there are many street vendors and beggars in the section up to the Parliament. With the *Oslo Pass (24 hours*

> **WHERE TO START?**
> **Operahuset:** Regardless of whether you arrive by ferry through Oslofjord or by car from Sweden, the Opera House **(U F5)** *(∭ f5)* is the perfect starting point as it is located both directly on the fjord and opposite the main station. Drive to one of the many multi-storey car parks near the railway station, walk across to the opera house and plan your stroll through the city from its accessible rooftop.

230 NOK | 48 hours 340 NOK | 72 hours 430 NOK | available from tourist information and other offices and under www.visitoslo.com) you can travel by bus and train free of charge, visit most of the main sights and use the municipal car parks.

SIGHTSEEING

AKERSHUS FESTNING OG SLOTT
(U D–E 5–6) (ლ d–e 5–6)

One of the most important medieval buildings in Norway lies on a promontory jutting out into the Oslofjord. Akershus was a fortress from 1319 to 1380 and transformed into a palace by King Christian IV at the beginning of the 17th century. Today, the castle is used for state receptions while the ● fortress complex is a favourite place for sun worshippers. *Fortress complex daily 6am–9pm | entrance free | castle (with royal mausoleum) beginning of May–Aug Mon–Sat 10am–4pm, Sun 12.30–4pm | entrance fee 65 NOK*

HENIE-ONSTAD-KUNSTSENTER ●
(0) (ლ 0)

In 1956, the Norwegian ice-skating princess Sonja Henie married the ship-owner Nils Onstadt and the couple established an art foundation in 1961. The Kunstsenter was opened in 1968 and houses – alongside the Louisiana in Denmark – the largest collection of modern art in Scandinavia. *Tue–Fri 11am–7pm, Sat/Sun 11am–5pm | entrance fee 80 NOK, free on Wed | www.hok.no | Høvikodden (12 km/7½mi west of Oslo) | motorway to Drammen | Bærum exit*

HOLMENKOLLEN ★ ● ⛷ (0) (ლ 0)

The 'mecca for Norwegian skiers' is dominated by the extremely modern main ski jump (record jump: more than 130 m/425 ft) that was opened in 2010. The view of the city, the fjord and the forests in the area is breathtaking. If you come here, you should also visit the *Ski Museum (in summer, daily 9am–8pm | entrance fee 90 NOK | www.holmenkollen.com | 8 km (5 mi) northwest of the city centre | Holmenkollen train from Majorstuen Station*

IBSENMUSEET (U C4) (ლ c4)

Henrik Ibsen's last apartment was opened as a museum exactly one hundred years after his death on 23 May 1906. The furnishings, colours and decoration were recreated and one gets a good impression of how Norway's world-famous playwright spent his twilight years. *Mid-May–mid-Sept daily 11am–6pm, other times Mon–Wed and Fri–Sun 11am–4pm, Thu 11am–6pm | entrance fee 85 NOK | Henrik Ibsens gate 26 | www.ibsenmuseet.no*

DET KONGELIGE SLOTT (U C3) (ლ c3)

The residence of the Norwegian royal family was erected between 1824 and 1828 in the Classicist style. The palace lies on an elevated site at the end of Karl Johans gate; the changing of the guard takes place at 1.30pm every day. The Palace Park is open to all. *Mid-June–mid-Aug tours in English Mon–Thu, Sat noon, 2 and 2.20pm Fri, Sun 2, 2.20 and 4 pm | entrance fee 95 NOK | www.kongehuset.no*

MUNCH-MUSEET (0) (ლ 0)

The gift of the famous Norwegian artist Edvard Munch (1863–1944) to his home town: around 1100 paintings, along with thousands of drawings and watercolours, graphic works and private correspondence. *June–Aug daily 10am–6pm, Sept–May Tue–Fri 10am–4pm, Sat, Sun 11am–5pm | entrance fee 75 NOK | Tøyengata 53 | www.munch.museum.no*

BYGDØY MUSEUM ISLAND
(U A6) (ლ a6)

The ideal destination to get your first impressions of Norway's history and culture

On display in the Kon-Tiki-Museum in Oslo: Thor Heyerdahl's papyrus boat Ra II

The *Fram-Museet (summer daily 9am–6pm, shorter opening hours at other times | entrance fee 60 NOK | www.fram.museum.no)* is devoted to a single ship. From 1892 onwards, the three-masted *Fram* (Forwards) was the expedition ship in which Fridtjof Nansen, Otto Sverdrup and Roald Amundsen set sail for the Arctic and Antarctic. You can see the adventurer and researcher Thor Heyerdahl's Kon-Tiki raft, the papyrus boat Ra II and a model of the Tigris in the *Kon-Tiki-Museum (in summer daily 9.30am–5.30pm, shorter opening hours at other times | entrance fee 65 NOK | www.kon-tiki. no)*. *Gjøa*, the yacht Roald Amundsen used to sail around North America between 1903 and 1905 belongs to the collection of the *Norsk Maritimtmuseum (mid-May–Aug daily 10am–6pm, shorter opening hours at other times | entrance fee 60 NOK | www.marmuseum.no)*. Three Viking ships that were found in burial mounds on the Oslofjord (especially impressive: the *Oseberg Ship*) can be seen in the *Vikingskipshuset (May–Sept daily 9am–6pm, shorter opening hours at other times | entrance fee 60 NOK | www.khm.uio.no/ vikingskiphuset)*. One hundred and seventy houses have been rebuilt in the *Norsk Folkemuseum (mid-May–mid-Sept daily 10am–6pm, shorter opening hours at other times | entrance fee 100 NOK | www. norskfolkemuseum.no)* to show how life was lived in Norway over the centuries. The oldest building is the *stave church from Gol* (around 1200).

NASJONALGALLERIET ⭐ (U D4) (🗺 d4)

The museum's holdings include 4,500 paintings, 1,500 sculptures and more than 40,000 drawings and pieces of graphic art. Works by Edvard Munch are on display along with the main 'Norwegian National Romanticism' exhibits. Temporary exhibitions of an international standard are held. *Tue, Wed, Fri 10am–6pm, Thu 10am–7pm,*

Sculptures in Vigelandsparken

RÅDHUSET (U D4) *(⍕ d4)*

With its two towers, the red-brick town hall that was built between 1930 and 1955 stands like a mighty gate between the harbour and inner city. Inside, you can see monumental paintings including works by Edvard Munch. *Daily 9am–6pm, tours daily in summer, Mon and Wed at other times 10am, noon and 2pm | free entrance*

VIGELANDSPARKEN ●
(U A1–2) *(⍕ a1–2)*

The complex with around 200 sculptures by Gustav Vigeland (1869–1943) is just one section of the vast Frognerpark that attracts around one million visitors annually – it is especially popular in summer. You should take your time walking up the avenue of stones leading to the ☆ *Monolith* and take in the aura of the figures that depict the cycle of life. From the upper end, you have a great view over the park and suburb of Frogner all the way to the city centre. *Open 24 hours a day | free entrance | main entrance Kirkeveien | www.vigeland museum.no*

Sat, Sun 11am–5pm | free entrance | Universitetsgata 13 | www.nasjonalmuseet.no

OPERAHUSET ★ (U F5) *(⍕ f5)*

The award-winning opera house on Bjørvika Bay is Oslo's new landmark: white marble, a magnificent interior and ● a roof with a ☆ panoramic view open to the public – a wonderful experience regardless of the weather. *Tours in English May Fri–Mon, June–15 Sept daily, Oct–Dec Sat, Sun 2pm | entrance 100 NOK | www.operaen.no*

FOOD & DRINK

THE BROKER

This inn serves the best hamburgers in town and perfectly tapped beer. *Bogstadveien 27 | tel. 22 93 04 80 | Budget*

INSIDER TIP ØSTKANTFOLK (0) *(⍕ 0)*

Reindeer, Arctic charr and smoked herring: here, the friendly staff serve traditional Norwegian cuisine in a living-room atmosphere. The eatery is located in the multicultural Grønland district. *Heimdalsgata 37 | tel. 91 10 09 95 | www.ostkantfolk.no | Budget–Moderate*

VILLA PARADISO (U F2) *(⍕ f2)*

Oslo's best pizza – naturally, baked in a stone oven from Naples. *Olav Ryes plass 8 tel. 22 35 40 60 | www.villaparadiso.no | Budget*

SHOPPING

Your stroll begins on *Karl Johans gate* (U D–E4) *(ⵍ d–e4)* where mainly international labels have their shops. The biggest shopping centres are near the main railway station with much more relaxed shopping at *Steen & Strøm (Nedre Slottsgate, at right angles to Karl Johan)* and *Paleet (Karl Johans gate 37)*. Fenaknoken *(www.fenaknoken.no)* (U D4) *(ⵍ d4)* on *Tordenskiolds gate* near the town hall sells Norwegian specialities such as dried fish, elk meat and goat's cheese. You will find small design and art shops on *Grünerløkka* (U F2–3) *(ⵍ f2–3)* on *Thorvald Meyers gate* (0) *(ⵍ 0)*. ☺ *Godt brød (Thorvald Meyers Gate 49)* bakes bread and cakes using organic ingredients only. The *skillingsboller* sprinkled with cinnamon and sugar are especially tasty.

SPORTS & ACTIVITIES

Visitors to Oslo who want to see something of the fjord and fjell landscape should make an excursion to *Nordmarka* (0) *(ⵍ 0)*. This gigantic recreation area starts at the Holmenkollen Ski Centre and surrounds the city like a green belt. There are 2,600 km (1,600 mi) of prepared cross-county trails where skiers and hikers can either stay overnight in cabins or just stop by for a rest.

ENTERTAINMENT

A stroll along fashionable *Aker Brygge* (U C5) *(ⵍ c5)*, in the *Frognerpark* (U A1–2) *(ⵍ a1–2)* or to Akershus Fortress is especially enjoyable on a summer evening. There are many café/clubs in *Grønland* (0) *(ⵍ 0)* and *Grünerløkka* (U F2–3)

(ⵍ f2–3) that serve Italian coffee in the afternoon, play rock music in the early evening and funk late at night. *Café Kaos (Thorvald Meyers gate 56)* (0) *(ⵍ 0)* in *Grünerløkka* has concerts (Wed), hits (Thu) and classics (Sat) – Fri is for chilling out! Things are much more tranquil in the *Tea Lounge (Thorvald Meyers gate 33)* where the music remains in the background but the mood is just as good.

WHERE TO STAY

BUDGET HOTEL OSLO (U E5) *(ⵍ e5)*
You can hardly stay anywhere that is more central and economical. Clean, respectable rooms, a simple breakfast and a slight youth-hostel feeling. Online bookings recommended. *55 rooms | Prinsensgate 6 | tel. 21 01 40 55 | www.olsobudgethotel.no | Budget*

COCHS PENSJONAT (U C3) *(ⵍ c3)*
Traditional family business near Palace Park, only a few minutes away from the palace itself. *88 rooms | Parkveien 25 | tel. 23 33 24 00 | www.cochspensjonat.no | Moderate*

INSIDER TIP ▶ **GJUSTEHUSET LOVISENBERG** (U E1) *(ⵍ e1)*
This guesthouse, built in 1878, is not right in the city centre but in the charming suburb of St Hanshaugen. It has been modernised but still takes its guests back to another age with its carefully restored furnishings and lamps and somewhat old-fashioned decor. There is only a television in the lounge. *32 rooms | Lovisenberggata 15a | tel. 22 35 83 00 | gjestehuset.lovisenberg.no | Budget*

HOLLMENKOLLEN PARK HOTEL ● ⚹⚹ (U F5) *(ⵍ f5)*
Heads of state are regular guests at this hotel – a wooden fairy-tale castle; a Swiss-

style architectural gem decorated with dragon heads. There is a view over the roofs of the city from the veranda. Furnishings, service, restaurant – everything is superlative. The spa adds the finishing touch to the perfect hotel experience. *220 rooms | Kongeveien 26 | tel. 22 92 20 00 | www. hollmenkollenparkhotel.no | Expensive*

INFORMATION

Trafikanten: Jernbanetorget 1 | tel. 81 53 05 55 (U F5) (🛒 f5); Turistinformasjon at the town hall: Fridtjof Nansens plass 5 (U D4) (🛒 d4) | www.visitoslo.com

WHERE TO GO

HEDDAL STAVKIRKE ★
(133 D4) (🛒 C17)

Norway's largest stave church is located right on the E34 near Notodden. It was built around 1200, has three naves and is noteable for its intricately carved porch with animal ornaments. The interior is richly decorated, including fine rose paintings. *May–Sept daily 10am–5pm, end of June–end of Aug 9am–7pm | entrance fee 60 NOK | www.heddalstavkirke.no*

KONGSBERG (133 D4) (🛒 C16)
The mining town (pop. 24,400) 82 km (51 mi) south-west of Oslo was founded in 1624 after silver was discovered there. In 1770, almost 10,000 people lived in the town; 4,000 of them worked in the silver mines including many miners from other parts of Europe. ● A trip in the 2.3 km-long (1½mi) *pit railway (mid–end of May, mid–end of Aug daily 11am, 1pm and 3pm, June–mid-Aug, hourly 11am–4pm | 150 NOK)*, followed by a one-hour tour of the mine tunnels, is a unique experience. *Information: Kongsberg Turistservice | Schwabesgate 2 (in the railway station) | tel. 32 29 90 50 | www.visitkongsberg.no*

TJØME (133 E5) (🛒 D–E17)
This narrow island that juts into the Skagerrak on the western side of Oslofjord is joined to the mainland by a bridge and is a popular destination for sun worshippers and gourmets. The famous guesthouse *Engø Gård (Gamlke Engø vei 25 | tel. 33 39 00 48 | www.engo.no | Expensive)* is located in a magnificent natural park. Those who prefer just to explore the island may well find themselves at ⚜ *Verdens Ende* – the end of the world. The mighty rock with a flashing beacon is the perfect place for courting couples to go for a walk on a summer's evening. *On the E18 to Tønsberg and then further to the south on Road 308 (130 km/80 mi from the centre of Oslo)*

TELEMARK

(132–133 C–D4) (🛒 B–C 16–17) **This region is considered the birthplace of skiing. And the forests are an endless paradise for hikers in summer. In addi-**

tion, the big lakes and extensive canals make a great variety of holiday experiences possible.

You can explore the Telemark region at leisure on board the two old ● **INSIDER TIP** steamers *Victoria* and *Henrik Ibsen* that depart from *Skien (133 D5) (m C17)* on the south coast in the morning and drop anchor in Dalen in the heart of the Telemark in the early evening. If you have a bicycle, the return journey along the banks of the Telemark Canal is the perfect finish to your active holiday. *Fare Skien–Dalen 600 NOK, return 300 NOK, bicycle 50 NOK | tel. 35 90 00 20 | www.visittelemark.no*

SIGHTSEEING

RJUKAN

This village (pop. 3600), that experienced a tremendous economic boom at the turn of the 20th century, lies wedged between two massive mountain ranges. Water power and sabotage activities against the German occupation forces are the focal points in the *Norwegian Industrial Workers' Museum (mid-June–mid-Aug daily 10am–6pm, shorter opening hours at other times | entrance fee 75 NOK | www.vistvemork. com | 5 km (3 mi) to the west | 15 minute walk from the car park).* The one-day walk to ☀ *Gaustatoppen* (1883 m/6178 ft) table mountain is rewarded with a panoramic view over much of southern Norway. *www.visitrjukan.com*

WHERE TO STAY

There are several spacious cabins to rent directly on the lake in the small village of *Vrådal (132 C5) (m C17)*; e.g. *Nisser Hyttesenter (5000 NOK per week | accommodates up to 8 | tel. 35 05 61 23 | www. hyttesenter.no).*

INFORMATION

Telemarkreiser AL | Nedre Hjellegate 18 | Skien | tel. 35 90 00 20 | www.visittele mark.no

A hiker's dream destination: the Telemark region is a great area for unwinding

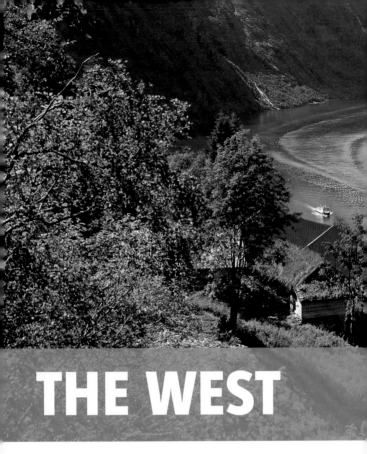

THE WEST

West Norway's frayed coastline is broken up by massive glacial inlets that extend right up to the rock faces of high mountains, forcing those coming overland to make lengthy detours.

But such detours can be fascinating, too: each one takes you to a different landscape, there are new surprises around every bend. West Norway is characterised by its dramatic countryside that provides a combination of relaxing and adventurous pursuits. Winter sports fans and hikers, water sports enthusiasts and anglers can all find the spot they are looking for between the glaciers and open sea, as can those who just want to discover the gems of Norway's cultural history in the great outdoors in the midst of a fascinating landscape.

ÅLESUND

(134 A5) (₥ B13) **The port (pop. 46,500) is surrounded by numerous islands and is the most important town – and a major centre of fishing – in the Sunnmøre fjord region.**

After the great fire in 1904 when – in a single day – 850 houses were razed to the ground and 10,000 people left homeless, the new town was reconstructed in

Photo: Geirangerfjord

Fjell, fjords and the coast: West Norway is fjord country – and still the firm favourite for Norway fans

the then modern Art Nouveau style. This was supported in part by the German Emperor Wilhelm II. In order to prevent any other conflagrations, stone was used instead of wood for building. The magnificent houses with their curved gables and other decorative elements are all located around the picturesque harbour whose canal-like branches divide the town centre.

SIGHTSEEING

AKSLA 🌿

The hill above Ålesund is not to be missed. You can either climb up the 418 steps to the top or follow the signs to *Fjellstua* in your car. You will be rewarded with a panoramic view over the town and its harbour, the neighbouring islands, sounds and the sea. And, to the south, the snow-

Open-air experience: the collection of historic houses in Sunnmøre Museum in Ålesund

capped peaks of the Sunnmøre Alps come into view – sheer magic!

JUGENDSTILSENTERET

An exhibition in the former Swan Chemists gives an impression of the architectural style that characterises Ålesund. The authentic furnishings make visitors feel they are back at the beginning of the 20th century. *June–Aug daily 10am–5pm | entrance fee 60 NOK | Apotekergata 16 | www.jugenstilsenteret.no*

SUNNMØRE MUSEUM

Around 50 old houses and 30 old boats, including Viking ships and a copy of a trading ship from the 11th century, can be seen in this open-air museum. *June–end of Aug Mon–Sat 11am–5pm, Sun noon–5pm, shorter opening hours at other times | entrance fee 70 NOK | Borgundgavlen | www.borgundgavlen.no | around 10 km (6¼mi) to the east of Ålesund*

FOOD & DRINK

SJØBUA

This is the place for excellent *bacalhau*. Although it is actually Portugal's national dish, the main ingredient – dried cod – comes from Norway. And dried cod has been produced in Ålesund for centuries. Another speciality is *flettafisk* – three fish are plaited together before being served. *Brunholmsgata 1a | tel. 70 12 71 00 | www.sjoebua.no | Expensive*

SHOPPING

DEVOLDFABRIKKEN ● ⚘

The factory on the other side of the fjord not only sells the Devold pullovers that are so popular with seafarers, it has extended its range to include sports and leisure clothing made by other manufacturers. A shop and a part of West-Norwegian industrial history, a café and a magnificent view of the islands outside Ålesund. *Ferry to Langevåg from the ZOB Quay (50 NOK)*

SPORTS & ACTIVITIES

KAYAK TOURS

The Storfjord, the 'Great Fjord', stretches inland from Ålesund – this is the perfect route for day-long excursions into the fjord world. If you didn't bring your kayak with you and would like to join a group, outdoor trips are organised by *Actin (tel. 92 09 57 45 | www.actin.no)*.

WHERE TO STAY

BORG BED & BREAKFAST

This B & B – a boarding school at other times of the year – lies 17 km (10½mi) to the east of Ålesund in beautiful surroundings on the way up the fjord. In the midst of a forest, you can see the peaks of the Sunnmøre Alps from the top of the next hill. The simple rooms are cosy and they all have their own bathroom; ten share a kitchen. *June–July | 45 rooms | Løypevegen 3 | tel. 70 17 76 00 | www.borgund.fhs.no | Budget*

HOTEL BROSUNDET

This hotel welcomes families and its guests can even prepare small meals. The rooms are rather functionally furnished but the gnarled beams give them a rustic, cosy touch. *47 rooms | Apotekergata 5 | tel. 70 11 45 00 | www.62nord.net | Expensive*

INFORMATION

Destinasjon Ålesund & Sunnmøre | Skateflukaia | tel. 70 15 76 00 | www.visit alesund.com

WHERE TO GO

GEIRANGERFJORD
★ (134 B6) (*∅ B14*)

The most famous destination and photo motive in West Norway: Geirangerfjord forces its way inland, surrounded by steep walls of rock, magnificent waterfalls and mountain massifs with hidden alpine farms.

You can reach the village of *Geiranger* by water from ↘ *Hellesylt* (80 km/50 mi south-east of Ålesund on Road 60) with the *car ferry (8 departures daily | ferry 140 NOK per person, car and driver 290 NOK)* or via a winding road. If you take *Road 63* from the south, the view from ↘ *Dalsnibba* (1450 m/4750 ft) (toll) will give you the first impression of what awaits visitors to Geirangerfjord. From Åndalsnes (134 B5) (*∅ B13*), the ↘ *Trollstigveien* hair-pin bends and the viewpoints in ↘ *Ørnesvingen* offer magnificent vistas of the Sunnmøre mountains. The most beautiful alternative route in this part of Norway leads to an idyllic valley and INSIDER TIP ▶ *Petrines Gyestgiveri (12 rooms | Norddal,*

MARCO POLO HIGHLIGHTS

Runde Island is the home of puffins

spend their summer here. The hike up to the ⚜ cliffs takes about one hour and you will not only be rewarded by the birds but also the magnificent view over the North Sea and the bracing ocean wind. Boat trips to the bird island depart from Ålesund. *75 km (47 mi) to the west of Ålesund | ferry from Sulasundet to Hareid (36 departures daily)*

BERGEN

(132 A3) (∅ A15) **Yes, it's true: Bergen has one of the highest rainfalls of any city on earth. But, when the sun does break through the clouds, all seats in the pavement cafés and restaurants are taken in a jiffy – no matter which direction the wind is blowing from or how cold it is.**

Bergen was founded in 1070 and today has a population of 251,000 making it Norway's second-largest city. It has a glorious past as a royal seat, a port and a member of the Hanseatic League. Bergen was the largest city in northern Europe in the Middle Ages. The Bryggen harbour quarter was in the hands of the Hansa from the 14th century and the last north-German merchants did not leave until 1764. The Bergen Card *(24 hours 200 NOK,*

Road 63 east of the Eidsdal ferry terminal | tel. 70 25 92 85 | www.petrines.com | Budget) – a guesthouse where you will feel at home and where blissful meals are served using the freshest of produce available (don't forget to try the strawberries). *www.geiranger.no*

GODØY (134 A5) *(∅ B13)*
Two underwater tunnels and a bridge lead to this small island off the coast of Ålesund. On the way, you can visit the island of *Giske* with its beautifully-located marble church from the 11th century. The ⚜ **INSIDER TIP** *Alnys fyr* lighthouse *(June–Aug, daily noon–6pm | tours 25 NOK)* that was erected on Godøy in 1936 is an important landmark. A café serves delicious home-made cakes and snacks.

RUNDE ★ (134 A5) *(∅ A13)*
The west of the island in the Ålesund shipping channel is a densely populated bird rock whose most important attraction are the hundreds of thousands of puffins that

> **CITY WHERE TO START?**
> **Fisketorget:** All paths lead to *Torgallmenning Square* and the *Fisketorget* (fish market) at the harbour. You should leave your car in a car park or – if you come from the south – near Bybanen station and take a train to the terminus in the city centre. If you arrive by sea on a ferry or Hurtigruten ship, follow signs to the closest multi-storey car park.

48 hours 260 NOK | available from the tourist information office, railway station and other places) offers a 30% reduction to the largest multi-storey car park, Bygarasjen, as well as free, or substantially reduced, entrance fees to most of the sights in the city. If you plan to stay overnight in summer, you should book your accommodation well in advance.

SIGHTSEEING

AKVARIET ●

You will not only be able to see local marine animals in West Norway's largest aquarium – crocodiles and snakes are also on display. Families with children will be delighted by the seals and penguins, and there is also a pool where you can put your hands in the water and really come into contact with the fish and crustaceans. *May–Aug daily 9am–7pm, at other times 10am–6pm | entrance fee 100 NOK | www.akvariet.no*

BERGEN KUNSTMUSEUM/
BERGEN KUNSTHALL

The three collections in the Kunstmuseum (Art Museum) on lake Lille Lungegårdsvann in the city cover a wide range: the permanent exhibition in the former municipal works *Lysverket* shows mainly Norwegian art from the Renaissance to the present day. The *Rasmus Meyers Samling* is principally devoted to Norwegian paintings, including works by Edvard Munch, Christian Krohg and Harriet Backer. As a rule, the *Stenersenbygget* concentrates on temporary exhibitions and frequently presents works by great masters. The fourth building, the *Bergen Kunsthall*, is reserved for temporary exhibitions of contemporary art. *'Museum Road' Rasmus Meyers alle | Bergen Art Museum: in summer daily 11am–5pm; at other times, closed Mon | entrance fee 80 NOK | www.bergen artmuseum.no | Bergen Kunsthall Tue–Sun noon–5pm | entrance fee 50 NOK, free on Fri 8–11pm | www.kunsthall.no*

BERGENSHUS FESTNING ☆

The *Håkonshalle*, built in 1261 in the Gothic style, is the heart of the Bergenshus fortress complex and is used today for concerts and other festive events. Construction of the neighbouring, massive *Rosary Tower* as a residence and defence installation was completed in 1568. *In summer daily 10am–4pm, shorter opening hours at other times | entrance fee 50 NOK | www.bymuseet.no*

Stroll through the old Hanseatic district of Bergen

BRYGGEN ★ ●

What is possibly the most famous district in Norway was in the hands of merchants from Lübeck for more than 400 years. Today, it is a Unesco World Heritage Site and just as lively as ever. A stroll through the old Hanseatic quarter, which was reconstructed after a major fire in 1702, could begin in the historic Finnegården courtyard of the *Hanseatic Museum (in summer, daily 9am–5pm, 11am–2pm at other times | entrance fee 50 NOK | www.museumvest.no)* and end in *Bryggens Museum (May–Aug daily 10am–6pm, shorter opening hours at other times | entrance fee 60 NOK | www.bymuseet.no)*. Between these two, you will be able to take a look at the last preserved – albeit reconstructed – *Shøtstue (included in the entrance fee for the Hanseatic Museum)* where the Hanseatic merchants held their meetings according to strict rules and enjoyed an evening drinking.

FISKETORGET (FISH MARKET)

In summer, there is a lot of pushing and shoving between the numerous fish stands every day; on Sat, many Bergeners come here to buy fresh fish, shrimps, fruit, vegetables and flowers. The goods are all of premium quality but the prices are somewhat higher than elsewhere. *June–Aug daily 7am–7pm, at other times Mon–Sat 7am–4pm | www.torgetibergen.no*

FLØYEN ☼

This lookout hill has a firm place in the hearts of the people of Bergen; it rises up 319 m (1050 ft) above the town centre and provides a magnificent view over the city and surrounding islands as far as the open sea. You can reach the summit in eight minutes with the *Fløiban (May–Aug Mon–Fri 7.30am–11.30pm, Sat 8am–11.30pm, Sun 9am–11pm, shorter opening hours at other times | fare 35 NOK for each direction | www.floibanen.no)*.

INSIDER TIP LEPRAMUSEET

This museum was established in a beautiful townhouse near the railway station. The building once housed the largest leper hospital in the country, St Jørgens Hospital. Norway's contribution to combating the disease – and especially that of the doctor Armauer Hansen – is the subject of the exhibition. *In summer daily 11am–3pm | entrance fee 50 NOK | St-Jørgens-Hospital | Kong Oscars gate 59 | www.bymuseet.no*

MARIAKIRKE

This house of worship, built around 1140 in the Romanesque style with its magnificent Baroque pulpit, lies a little bit outside Bryggen. St Mary's Church was used by the Hanseatic merchants for their religious services from 1408–1766. *Mid-*

You will feel transported back to the days of the Hansa in Enhjørningen Restaurant

June–mid-Aug Mon–Fri 9.30–11.30am and 1–4pm, at other times 11am–12.30pm | entrance fee 20 NOK | Dreggen

FOOD & DRINK

INSIDER TIP ▶ CAFÉ OPERA

Even the locals ask themselves how it is possible that this small café-restaurant has managed to remain so popular for almost three decades. One of the reasons is its location between the university and city centre, a second is the short menu with excellent dishes, and a third is the wish to provide a stage for musicians and artists and, in this way, keep the guests entertained. *Valkendorfsgate 1B | Budget*

ENHJØRNINGEN/TO KOKKER

Bergen's best fish dishes are served in *Enhjørningen* in the Hanseatic Enjhørnings-gården courtyard in Bryggen. To kokker in the same house specialises in meat dishes. *Enhjørningen tel. 55 30 69 50 | To kokker tel. 55 30 69 55 | www.enhjorningen. no | Expensive*

SHOPPING

Galleriet (Torgallmenning) in the centre of town has a total of almost 60 shops under a single roof. You will be able to buy arts and crafts in the small shops on *Lille Øvregate* to the right of the Fløibanen; the Bergen branch of *Husfliden (www.norskflid. no/bergen)* is located directly behind the Tourist Information Office. Strandkaien opposite Bryggen is the site of the following two shops: *Vågen Fetevarer* has the best lamb and *Strandkalen Fisk* is the right place to go for warm *fiskekaker*.

ENTERTAINMENT

You will soon realise that Bergen is a town with a great many students and an international, innovative music scene if you visit concerts in the *Garage (Christies gate 14 | www.garage.no)* and *Det Akademiske Kvarteret (Olv Kyrres gate 14 | www.kvarteret)*. It is a lot of fun to visit some of Bergen's café clubs in the early evening – later, it can be less pleasant. You should try to avoid *Torgallmenning* in the centre of town late at night – where the more negative aspects of high-proof fun and games can be witnessed.

HENRIK ØL & VINSTUE

This is the perfect place to start your evening in Bergen. An extensive selection of British, German and Norwegian beers, not too much noise and nice people in front of – and behind – the bar. *Engen 10*

PINGVINEN

Absolutely trendy – because of the relaxed atmosphere, the extensive list of beers and the traditional Norwegian food (*Budget*). *Vaskerelven 14 | tel. 55 60 46 46*

HOTEL ADMIRAL ⁂

Today, what was once a harbour warehouse is the hotel with the best view. Soft colour schemes have been used in the rooms, some of which are quite small; the service is exceptional. *210 rooms | C. Sundtsgate 9 | tel. 55 23 64 00 | www. clarionadmiral.no | Expensive*

JACOBS APARTMENT & HOTEL

The perfect place for those who want to take care of themselves; centrally located between the railway station and centre of town. The rooms and flats are tastefully furnished but somewhat expensive in the summer season. The ☺ restaurant on the ground floor serves organic food and wines. *21 rooms | Kong Oscars gate 44 | tel. 55 54 41 60 | www.jacobsbergen. no | Moderate*

SKANSEN PENSJONAT

This small guesthouse, run on an ecologically-friendly basis and where guests soon feel at home, lies just a few steps up from Fløibanen in the centre of town. *7 rooms,*

1 flat | Vetrlidsallmenningen 29 | tel. 55 31 90 80 | www.skansen-pensjonat.no | Moderate

Turistinformasjon | Vågsallmenningen 1 | tel. 55 55 20 00 | www.visitbergen.no

LYSØEN (132 A3) (*𝄞 A16*)

Its rustic mix of styles makes the country home of Bergen's miraculous violinist Ole Bull (1810–88) on a small island in Fanafjord well worth seeing. The visit comes along with a short boat trip. *In summer, Mon–Sat noon–4pm, Sun 11am–5pm | entrance fee 30 NOK, incl. guided tour, boat transfer 60 NOK | 25 km (15½mi) south of Bergen on Road 553*

TROLDHAUGEN/GRIEG MUSEUM AND HOME (132 A3) (*𝄞 A15*)

For 22 years, this villa on a promontory in Nordåsvannet Lake was the home of Edvard Grieg and his wife Nina between spring and summer. The small cabin near the water that Grieg used for composing inspired him to many world-famous works. Concerts are held regularly in summer in the well-hidden Troldsalen between the villa and museum. *May–Sept daily 9am–6pm | entrance fee 60 NOK | Troldhaugveien 65 | 10 km (6¼mi) south of Bergen | www. troldhaugen.com | take the Bybanen 'light rail' tram (alight at Hop)*

HARDANGER

(132 B–C 3–4) (*𝄞 B15–16*)   The **Folgefonna Glacier towers over the region to the side of the Hardangerfjord that extends inland to the south of Bergen as far as the high Hardangervidda plateau.**

No matter where you look: waterfalls plummet from the snow-covered heights to the valley. Hundreds of thousands of fruit trees grow between the forested slopes and the fjord that shimmers a bluish-green in summer. The blossoming fruit trees at the end of April – when people are still skiing just a few hundred metres further up the slope – are an absolute highlight.

SIGHTSEEING

HARDANGER-FARTØYVERNSENTERET (HARDANGER MUSEUM SHIPYARD)

This is where schooners, sailing boats and even old rowing boats are made shipshape once again. Visitors can also learn something about the craft of the rope-maker. Guided tours in summer; café. *May–early Sept daily 10am–5pm | entrance fee 80 NOK | Norhelmsund | www.fartoyvern.no*

HARDANGERVIDDA ⭐

This is the largest high-altitude plateau in Europe, extending over an area of 9000 km² (3475 mi²), and is the Norwegian

hiking area *per se*. The well-marked paths that criss-cross the barren, 1000 to 1600 m (3200–5200 ft)-high plateau are only clearly distinguishable between June and September. The flora is limited to stunted birch trees, grass and lichen but the fauna has many surprises in store: birds of prey, lemmings and Europe's most southerly reindeer herds. The only real peaks are in the west; hiking is completely safe and nights can be spent in self-catering cabins or professionally run accommodation, or even in your own tent. The best places to start your hike on the 'Viddda' are Road 7 on the northern border and the E 134 on the south-eastern periphery near *Røldal*. A strenuous but beautiful climb ends at ⚜ *Munkentrappene* near *Loftus* (Road 13) on the western border of the Hardangervidda, the route having been constructed by monks in the 13th century. An even more dramatic climb is from Kinsarvik through *Husedalen*, the 'Valley of the Waterfalls'.

HARDANGERVIDDA NATURCENTER

Those who are not able to discover all Hardangervidda has to offer on a hike can

Loosen up – in the barren landscape of the Hardangervidda

get a detailed overview of the natural and cultural history of the plateau at this centre. The kitchen staff in the *restaurant (tel. 53 66 59 00 | Budget)* conjure up excellent traditional meals. *April–Oct daily 10am–6pm, 15 June–20 Aug 9am–8pm | entrance fee 120 NOK | www.hardangervidda.org | Øvre Eidfjord*

Maritime elegance on the fjord: Rica Seilet Hotel in Molde

VØRINGFOSSEN ★ ☀

You will hardly be able to see all the way down to the bottom of this easily accessible waterfall but the view over the thundering water and deep gorge is all the more exciting. Every second, 12 m³ (424 ft³) of water plummet into the ravine that is full of small rainbows. Gigantic ☀ *Sysendamm* is located just a few miles away towards the Hardangervidda. There you

will have a wonderful view of the valley and Hardangerjøkulen Glacier.

STEINSTØ FRUKTGARD ☀

This café serves fruit and berries from Hardanger, Norwegian home-style cooking – and a breathtaking view over the fjord and fjell. *Fykesundvegen | Steinstø (on Road 7) | tel. 56 55 79 33 | www.steinstofruktgard.no | Budget*

INSIDER TIP ▶ VILTKROA

Organic gourmet meals at a camping site: Trout, reindeer and lots of veggies. *Måbødalen Camping | Øvre Eidfjord | tel. 53 66 59 88 | www.mabodalen.no | Moderate*

WHERE TO STAY

HARDANGER GJESTEGARD

A former fruit press forms the core of this orchard guesthouse where the machines and wine cellar have been preserved. *7 rooms | tel. 97 10 18 78 | www.hardanger-gjestegard.no | Alsåker | Utne | Moderate*

INFORMATION

Reisemål Hardangerfjord | Norheimsund | tel. 56 55 38 70 | www.hardangerfjord.com

MOLDE

(134 B5) (ɯ B13) **The small town (pop. 19,500) on the fjord of the same name is the administrative centre of the Møre og Romsdal district.**

Everything goes really overboard at the summer Jazz Festival in the 'City of Roses'. The surrounding countryside has a lot to offer with its exciting juxtaposition of mountains, fjords and the open sea. There is a splendid view of the Romsdalen peaks from the more modest Varden Mountain (407 m, 1350 ft) on the northern outskirts of the town.

SIGHTSEEING

ROMSDALSMUSEET

You can visit around 50 old buildings in this idyllically located open-air museum above the town centre. *June, Aug Mon–Sat 11am–3pm, Sun noon–3pm, July Mon–Sat 11am–6pm, Sun noon–6pm | entrance fee 70 NOK | www.romsdalsmuseet.no*

SHOPPING

DEN GODE SMAK

Exclusive traditional and delicatessen produce can be bought here directly from Norwegian farms. *Torget 1*

SPORTS & ACTIVITIES

INSIDER TIP ▶ CYCLING BY THE SEA

Discover the islands off the coast of Molde by bike. You will hardly ever be bothered by cars as you make your way from one island to the next; there will be the taste of salt on your lips and a peaceful bay around the next bend. The tour over three islands, starting in Molde, is 200 km (125 mi) long.

WHERE TO STAY

YZ HUSTADVIKA GJESTEGÅRD

This guesthouse, built on the ruins of a fish trading post, is located in Farstad, about 50 km (31 mi) to the north of Molde. *17 rooms, 14 cabins | Storholmen | tel. 71 26 47 00 | www.hustadvika.no | Moderate*

RICA SEILET HOTEL ☼

In Molde, directly on the fjord, shaped like an enormous sail. Most of the rooms have magical views. *222 rooms | tel. 71 11 40 00 | www.rica.no | Expensive*

INFORMATION

Turistinformasjon | Torget 4 | tel. 71 20 10 00 | www.visitmolde.com

WHERE TO GO

BUD AND ATLANTIC OCEAN ROUTE ●
(134 B4–5) (*ØØ B12–13*)

This route starts in the idyllic fishing village of Bud and proceeds northwards along the Hustadvika section of the coast that was feared by seafarers on account of its unpredictable winds and currents – and, you can be assured that you will still have close contact with the elements! You travel over eight bridges that connect small islands and skerries with each other to the island of *Averøya* and further on to the port of *Kristiansund*. There are places to stop and have a rest – and even go fishing – to the left and right of the road. *www.visitkristiansund.com*

SOGNEFJORD

(132 A–C2) (*ØØ A–B 14–15*) **This gigantic estuary and towering mountains on both sides characterize Norway's longest and deepest fjord.**

Even today, travellers have to rely on the ferries that cross the fjord at all times of the day. Some of the side arms of the Sognefjord are famous tourist attractions created by Mother Nature. The Aurlandsfjord and Nærøyfjord – one of the narrowest navigable fjords – are Unesco World Heritage Sites.

SIGHTSEEING

BALESTRAND

The countryside and the light have attracted artists to this small village at the widest point of Sognefjord for 150 years.

Peace and quiet reign between the pretty houses — including some galleries — and the view over the fjord is unsurpassed. You can spend the night in *Kviknes Hotel (190 rooms | tel. 57 69 42 00 | www.kviknes. no | Expensive)* a fairy-tale hotel in the Swiss style whose reception rooms also function as a museum.

The INSIDER TIP *ferry from Balestrand to Fjærland (May–Sept daily 11.50am, June–Aug also 8.05 am)* steers northwards through *Fjærlandfjord* directly towards an arm of *Jostedalsbreen*, the largest glacier on the European continent.

BORGUND STAVKIRKE ⭐ ●

The most famous of Norway's stave churches (built around 1180) is on the E16 30 km (19 mi) to the east of Lærdal, a small town at the eastern end of Sognefjord. The dragon heads on the gable and wonderful carvings on the west entrance are especially striking. If there are too many tourists, it can be worth changing your plans and visiting the stave church in Undredal. *May–mid-June and mid-Aug–Sept daily 10am–5pm, mid-June–mid-Aug 8am–8pm | entrance fee 70 NOK | www. stavechurch.com*

FLÅMSBANA ⭐

The village of *Flåm* is located at the foot of Aurlandsfjord and is the end station of the Flåms railway line that starts 20 km (12½ mi) to the south in *Myrdal (865 m/ 2870 ft)*, and winds its way breathtakingly past the towering, rocky precipices of the Flåmsdalen and through tunnels until it reaches the shore of the fjord. *Fare 340 NOK | tours from Bergen | www.flaams bana. no*

NORSK BREMUSEUM

This architecturally interesting museum focuses on Jostedalsbreen Glacier and includes exhibitions, models and a wide-screen film. It is located in Fjærland at the foot of the Bøyabreen and Suphellebreen glacier arms. *April–May and Sept–Oct 10am–4pm, June–Aug 9am–7pm | entrance fee 110 NOK | www.bre.museum.no*

STEGASTEINEN ☀

This 4-metre-wide and 30-metre-long footbridge of wood and steel juts out into space 650 m (2133 ft) above Aurlandsfjord. Anybody who dares walk out there is rewarded with a unique panoramic view of the fjord landscape. *On the Aurlandsvegen pass road between Aurland and Lærdal, turn off shortly after Aurland*

INSIDER TIP UNDREDAL STAVKIRKE

The smallest church in Scandinavia lies hidden between the gigantic mountain scenery on the shore of Aurlandfjord 13 km (8 mi) to the north of Flåm. The church is only 4 metres wide and was probably built in the 12th century. The

village of Undredal is also famous for its goat's cheese.

Balestrand Turistinformasjon | Kaien | tel. 57 69 12 55; Fjærland Turistkontor | tel. 57 69 32 33; Gaupne Turistkontor | tel. 97 60 04 43 | Breheimsenteret Jostedal | tel. 57 68 32 50; Sogndal Turistkontor | Hovevegen 2 | tel. 97 60 04 43; www.sognefjord. no | www.air.no (Aurland, Lærdal, Flåm)

WHERE TO GO

NORDFJORD (132 B1) (*m B14*)

Pretty villages and high hills that invite tourists to take long hikes lie on both sides of Nordfjord beneath the gigantic Jostedalsbreen glacier. Trips to the Briksdalsbreen glacier snout *(mid-April–mid-Oct daily 6.15pm | bookings tel. 57 87 68 05 | 170 NOK | www.oldedalen-skysslag.com).*

start in the *Oldedalen Valley* 22 km (14 mi) after the signposted turnoff in Olden (185 km/116 mi north of Balestrand). A more economical alternative is to travel along the Loenvatnet Lake from Loen to the end of Kjenndal Valley. From there, it is only a fifteen-minute walk to the Kjenndalsbreen glacial arm. *Further Information: Reisemål Stryn & Nordfjord | tel. 57 87 40 40 | www.nordfjord.no*

STADLANDET/VESTKAPP
(132 A–B1) (*m A–B 13–14*)

Ships depart for the ruins of the *Selje Monastery (departures: July daily, June/ Aug twice daily | 180 NOK | tickets from the Tourist Information Office | tel. 57 85 66 06 | www.seljekloster.no)* from the harbour at *Selje (245 km/155 mi from Balestrand).* The monastery was erected by Benedictine monks at the beginning of the 12th century in honour of St Sunniva, the patron saint of West Norway. You will discover a

Icy barrier: Nordfjord is ideal for long hikes

STAVANGER

wonderful bathing beach in *Ervik* below Vestkapp. *Vestkapp Camping (cabins for 4 or 6 | tel. 57 85 99 50 | www.vestkapp camping.com | Budget)* at the turn off to the village is the perfect starting point for a trip to  Vestkapp that is a mere 3 km away. The almost 500-metre-high rock towers over the Stadlandet coast that is feared for its changing winds and currents.

STAVANGER

(132 B5) *(ɯ A17)* **Norway's oil capital (pop. 119,000) is an exciting mixture of old and new.**
Life in the streets in the old town *(Gamle Stavanger)* to the west of Vågen harbour bay is quite peaceful while the shore on the other side is characterised by streets of shops, bars and restaurants.

SIGHTSEEING

NORSK HERMETIKKMUSEUM

The Canning Museum in an old factory that used to be used for this purpose gives an impression of the history of Stavanger in the days when it was an important fishing and fish-processing centre. *15 June–15 Aug daily 11am–4pm, at other times 11am–4pm | entrance fee 60 NOK | Øvre Strandgate 88 | www.stavanger. museum.no*

NORSK OLJEMUSEUM

The interactive oil museum shows how black gold evolves and is used and how the offshore adventure has transformed Norway. *June–Aug daily 10am–7pm, Sept– May Mon–Sat 10am–4pm, Sun 10am– 6pm | entrance fee 80 NOK | Kjering- holmen | www.norskolje.museum.no*

Digging for (black) gold: Norsk Oljemuseum in Stavanger

FOOD & DRINK

BEVAREMEGVEL

The name is a figure of speech – something along the lines: 'you must be joking!' Varied lunch menu, daily specials until 6pm. *Skagen 12 | tel. 51 84 38 60 | www.herlige-restauranter.no/bevaremegvel | Expensive*

SHOPPING

INSIDER TIP JANS FISKERØYKERI ☺

This is the home of Norway's best smoked salmon that is produced here in chambers from the post-war years. Gourmets from all over Europe regularly come to stock up on gravlax or smoked salmon. *Johannes gate 37*

BEACHES

Thanks to the Ice Age and Gulf Stream: there are wonderful sandy beaches with dunes for sunbathing near Stavanger.

ORRESTRANDA

The Jæren beaches start south of Sola Airport. The most delightful are *Borestranda* (around 15 km/9½ mi south of the airport) and *Orrestranda* (22 km/14 mi to the south).

INSIDER TIP SANDVESTRANDEN

This sandy beach, surrounded by cliffs, that offers a magnificent view of the North Sea and where there is even plenty of room on warm summer days lies a little to the north of the picturesque harbour town Skudeneshavn on Karmøy (22 km/14 mi north of Stavanger; ferry).

ENTERTAINMENT

It is really lively on the quay and in the small streets on the northern side of Vågen Bay; there is plenty of action until closing time (clubs at 3.30am; other venues 2am). *The Cardinal Pub & Bar (closed Mon | Skagen 21)* has Norway's largest selection of beer with more than 500 varieties. Really full after 9pm and always a good atmosphere.

WHERE TO STAY

FIRST HOTEL ALSTOR

A modern building with spacious, classically decorated rooms. The evening buffet is included in the price of the room. 2 km (1.2 mi) from the centre of town. *81 rooms | Tjensvollveien 31 | tel. 42 04 40 00 | www.firsthotels.com | Moderate*

SOLA STRAND HOTEL ●

This peaceful oasis lies to the south, near the airport. The white building, constructed in 1914, the dunes, sky and sea, all combine to create a harmonious whole. With spa, swimming pool and sauna. *90 rooms | Axel Lundsvei 47 | Sola | tel. 51 94 30 00 | www.sola-strandhotel.no | Expensive*

INFORMATION

Turistinformasjon | Domkirkeplassen 3 | tel. 51 85 92 00 | www.regionstavanger.com

WHERE TO GO

LYSEFJORD ★ ● 〰
(132 B5) (*∅ A–B17*)

You can reach this extremely narrow fjord by *excursion boat (July–Aug daily 10.30am and 2.30pm, at other times daily noon from Skagen Quay | journey time 3 hours | 380 NOK)*. During this trip you will be able to admire the famous *Preikestolen* (The Pulpit) rocky plateau from below. Or you can take the *Stavanger–Tau Ferry (40 min | around 30 departures daily)* and then drive on Road 13 to *Jøssang* where the hike to the plateau begins (allow around two hours).

TRØNDELAG

The area around the cathedral and university city of Trondheim offers a variety of stunning scenery.

The mountains in the south are popular places for skiing and hiking. The Trondheimsfjord with its various arms is bordered by pasture land through which some of the best salmon rivers in the country wind their way. But, above all, Trøndelag is an eldorado for anyone interested in history.

DOVREFJELL

(134–135 C–D 5–6) (*C13–14*) **The Dovrefjell mountain region with the** national park of the same name is the gateway to Trøndelag.

The E6 makes its way through the mountain range where 2500 wild reindeer and 130 musk oxen roam. Botanists are attracted by the richness of the plant life that can be found here and geologist are fascinated by the moraines and other deposits that were formed during the last Ice Age. The most important town in the region, *Oppdal*, is popular with families with children.

SIGHTSEEING

The *Kongsvold Fjeldstue* (www.kongsvold. no) hotel has a long history as a mountain

Photo: The old city bridge in Trondheim

The region around Trondheim: a weather-beaten coastline, a fertile hinterland and the centre of Norway's ecclesiastical history

guesthouse and is, at the same time, also a station for botanic and zoological research. The snow-capped, 2286 m (7500 ft)-high peak of 🔆 **INSIDER TIP** *Snøhetta* is the goal of a seven-hour hike through the realm of the musk oxen. It is even better if you take part in a *Musk Oxen Safari (from Kongsvold Fjeldstue or the Dombås Tourist Office | duration: around 5 hours | price 300 NOK | www.moskus-safari.no).*

Kongsvoll is 43 km (33 mi) north of Dombås on the E6

WHERE TO STAY

HJERKINN FJELLSTUE
A rustic hotel that also offers many leisure activities on the treeline at an altitude of 1000 m (3300 ft). *38 rooms | tel. 612151 00 | www.hjerkinn.no | Moderate–Expensive*

RØROS

(135 D5) *(ω D13)* ⭐ **Time seems to have come to a standstill in the former copper-mining community (pop. 3600) near the Swedish border.**

The church – the only stone building as far as the eye can see – towers above the rows of around 50 listed houses on the

The Rørosmuseet with models from the world of copper mining

two main streets. Røros is a winter-holiday resort: the temperature can sink to minus 30°C (–22°F) but, in this dry inland climate, a sleigh ride is still a great experience.

SIGHTSEEING

OLAVSGRUVA (OLAV'S PIT)

This copper mine is located around 13 km (8 mi) east of Røros on Road 31 towards the Swedish border. *Tours 20 June–15 Aug daily 10.30am, noon, 2, 3.30 and 5pm, June–Sept Mon–Sat 1 and 3pm, Sun noon | entrance fee 90 NOK | www.rorosmuseet.no*

INSIDER TIP ▸ RØROSMUSEET

An excellent museum that uses models to give you an idea of how a mine functions. It is on the outskirts of town next to the gigantic slag heaps. *20 June–15 Aug daily 10am–6pm, at other times Mon–Fri 11am–4pm, Sat/Sun 11am–3pm | entrance fee 70 NOK | www.rorosmuseet.no*

FOOD & DRINK

VERTSHUSET RØROS

Traditional meat dishes served in an exceptional atmosphere compensates for high prices. *Kjerkgata 34 | tel. 72 41 93 50 | www.vertshusetroros.no | Expensive*

WHERE TO STAY

VINGELS GAARD GJESTGIVERI

Rustic mountain guesthouse at an altitude of 750 m (2500 ft) with alpine pastures and a magnificent hiking area that is also perfect for mountain bikers. *8 rooms | Gardsjordet | Vingelen | tel. 62 49 48 20 | www.vingelsgaard.no | Moderate*

TRONDHEIM

(135 D4) *(∅ D12)* **Until the Reformation, Trondheim (pop. 160,000) was the seat of the Norwegian archbishop and a centre of pilgrimage, it being presumed that the cathedral was built on the site of Saint Olav's tomb.**

The *Nidarosdomen* is Norway's only cathedral and the most important sight in a city that is best know today for its University of Technology and internationally-renowned research institutions – this makes it not at all surprising that WiFi is available free of charge in the city centre *(www.tradlose trondheim.no)*.

SIGHTSEEING

ERKEBISPEGÅRDEN

The archbishop's palace was the political and spiritual centre from the middle of the 12th century but, after the Reformation, became the residence of the North Norwegian feudal lords and later a military depot. Archaeological finds, religious sculptures and weapons are on display here. *May–14 Sept Mon–Fri 10am–3pm (in summer, 5pm), Sat 10am–3pm, Sun noon–4pm, shorter opening hours at other times | entrance fee 50 NOK or 100 NOK including Nidarosdomen and the crown jewels*

DAMLE BYBRO (OLD CITY BRIDGE)

This bridge was built in 1861 and leads from the city centre to the *Bakklandet* district with its narrow streets and pretty INSIDER TIP wooden houses. The Trondheimers lovingly call the red superstructure the 'Door to Happiness'.

MUNKHOLMEN ★ ⚘

A small island in the fjord facing the city with very well preserved monastic ruins. This is where chiefs were beheaded in

CITY **WHERE TO START?**
Nidarosdomen: The cathedral is both your first destination and starting point. You can reach it by car via the E6. Coming from the south, turn off into the Lade suburb and park at the *City Syd Shopping Centre* from where there is a regular bus service to the centre. From the north, follow signs to the centre and drive to the *Leuthenhaven multi-storey car park (Erling Skakkes gate 40, closed Sun)*.

Viking days; from 1658, the monastery, which was erected at the beginning of the 11th century, was used as a fortress and prison. There are delightful views of the city and fjord from bathing places on the island. *Ferry, in summer daily, every hour 10am–6pm (return fare 55 NOK) from Ravnkloa dock by the fish hall*

NIDAROSDOMEN ★

The original cathedral was founded around 1070 but frequent fires destroyed large

★ Røros
A journey back in time to the heyday of copper mining → p. 66

★ Munkholmen
Small island facing Trondheim with a 'captivating' past → p. 67

★ Nidarosdomen
Cathedral and Norway's coronation church → p. 67

★ Ringve Museum
Lovely building in Trondheim housing the Music Museum → p. 68

MARCO POLO HIGHLIGHTS

The magnificent nave in Nidaros Cathedral in Trondheim

RINGVE MUSEUM ★

Ringve Gård manor house from the 18th century lies in a magnificent park on the eastern outskirts of the city and is now the site of a music museum. It is even possible to play some of the instruments in the collection exhibited in a renovated barn. *Mid-April–end of June and end of Aug–mid-Sept daily 11am–4pm, end of June–end of Aug 11am–5pm | entrance fee 80 NOK | Lade suburb | www.ringve.no*

Stiftsgården (Monastery Garden)
The 58 m (190 ft) long city court was completed in 1778 and the rooms and furnishings are characteristic of the Rococo period. When walking through the halls, visitors have the feeling that they are promenading through a wooden palace. *June–20 Aug Mon–Sat 10am–5pm, Sun noon–5pm (tours every hour) | entrance fee 60 NOK | Munkegata 23*

TYHOLT-TÅRNET (TELEVISION TOWER) ⬆

A perfect view of Trondheim and its surroundings from a height of 120 m (394 ft). The tower restaurant *Egon (Moderate)*, 80 m (262 ft) above the ground, serves pizzas and good luncheon dishes. *Otto Nielsens vei 4*

VITENSKAPSMUSEUM

The Museum of Science shows archeological finds from the Stone Age to the Viking period. Rewarding exhibitions on medieval Trondheim and religious art to around 1700. *Tue–Fri 10am–4pm, Sat/Sun 11am–4pm | entrance fee 30 NOK | Erling Skakkes gate 47 | www.ntnu.no/vitenskapsmuseet*

FOOD & DRINK

DICKENS

Bistro with grilled foods and delicious snacks. *Kjøpmannsgata 57 | tel. 73 51 57 50 | Moderate*

sections of this national monument. In 1869, the increase in national self-awareness led to its comprehensive renovation that was not completed until 100 years later. The return of the crown jewels in 1988 confirmed the position of the cathedral as the coronation church. The ⬆ tower is a perfect vantage point. *May–14 Sept Mon–Fri 9am–3pm (mid-June–beginning of Aug 9am–5.30pm), Sat 9am–2pm, Sun 1–4pm | entrance fee 50 NOK | www.nidarosdomen.no*

DEN GODE NABO

This cosy pub is in the cellar beneath the exclusive *Bryggen* restaurant next to the city bridge. Øvre Bakklandet 66 | tel. 40 61 88 09 | www.dengodenabo.com | *Budget*

SHOPPING

There are rows of art galleries, cafés, antique and designer shops in the Bakklandet quarter. Husfliden (www.norskfliden.no/ trondheim) has a branch at *Tryggvasons gate 18*.

ENTERTAINMENT

Trondheim is more of a students' town than a metropolis. Being too stylish is completely out of place, beer – not champagne – is the order of the day. If you want to dance to loud music (often live) *Brukbar (Munkegata 26)* in the city centre is the place to go.

WHERE TO STAY

CLARION COLLECTION HOTEL BAKERIET

This elegantly decorated hotel, with cheerful, comfortable rooms is located away from traffic but is still in the centre. 109 rooms | Brattørgata 2 | tel. 73 99 10 00 | www.choicehotels.no | *Expensive*

COMFORT HOTEL PARK

Its position next to the cathedral means that this modern centrally located hotel is comparatively quiet. The hotel also serves organic alternatives at breakfast. 210 rooms | Prinsensgate 4A | tel. 73 83 39 00 | www.choicehotels.no | *Moderate*

SINGSAKER SOMMERHOTELL

The largest wooden residential building in all Scandinavia is actually a students' hostel in a green area close to the centre. There are rooms with one to four beds, some of them with a private shower. Mid-June–mid-Aug | 104 rooms | Rogertsgate 1 | tel. 73 89 31 00 | sommerhotell.singsaker.no | *Budget*

INFORMATION

Turistinformasjon | Torvet | tel. 73 80 76 60 | www.trondheim.com

WHERE TO GO

HEGRA FESTNING (135 D4) (*D12*)

This fortress near the Swedish border was constructed in 1905 when Norway dissolved its union with Sweden. The complex with its weapons has been entirely preserved and is located in a lovely woody area which is also a delightful place to go for a walk. June–Aug Mon–Sat 11am–4pm, Sun 11am–5pm, shorter opening hours at other times | entrance fee 80 NOK | www. hegrafestning.no | around 50 km (31 mi) east of Trondheim | turn off the E6 to the E14 near Stjørdal, follow signs from Hegra

LOW BUDGET

▶ There is free entrance to many events at the *Olavfesttagen (end of July/early August)* in Trondheim.

▶ Hikers through the hills of North Trøndelag will find cosy accommodation at *Føllingstua Camping Site* 14 km (8½mi) north of Steinkjer. 4 people, 490 NOK a night | tel. 74 14 71 90 | www.follingstua.no

▶ Entrance is free to the *Norwegian Museum of Justice*, the *Resistance Museum* and the *Armament Museum* in Trondheim, as well as the *Botanical Gardens* in Ringve and *Tyholt Tower*.

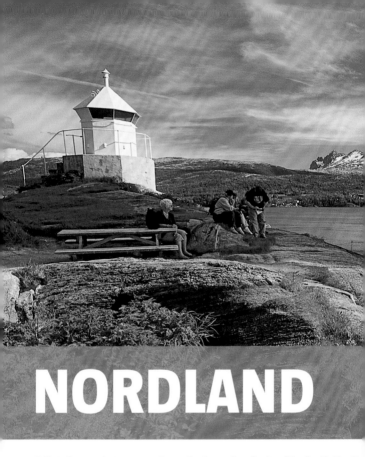

NORDLAND

At first glance, what opens up beyond Trondheim is just an endlessly long, narrow stretch of land. But this soon turns out to be one of the most beautiful and varied regions in Norway to those who are prepared to take a closer look.

The narrowest piece of Norway is located in the *fylke* Nordland – it is a mere 6 km (3¾ mi) from the end of the Tysfjord to the Swedish border.

Only two roads make their way northwards: one, through a densely forested valley and the other, with the help of numerous ferries, along the coast. If you take the main road to the north, the E6, you will need almost an entire day to drive from the southern border of Nordland to Narvik. So just pull over to the right and let this region – already arctic in character – charm you with all that it has to offer: nature galore.

Nordland is the homeland of Knut Hamsun; this is where the poet and Nobel Prize laureate created and settled many of the characters in his books. They live from fishing and love their Nordland, cheerful stories and crude jokes. The Nordlanders are always full of respect when they talk about the weather and do not let themselves be put down by the whims of nature or by the high and mighty. It will also not take you very long to find out just how

Tarry awhile: a small strip of land, hospitable people and an incredibly beautiful mass of islands

warm-hearted the people here can be. Although Nordland is small, it is big enough for many a holiday and a trip with the Hurtigruten ships along the coast of Helgeland is the beginning of an intense relationship for many. Alpine lakes lie hidden behind the boulders of the eastern Satfjell Mountains and there are massive glaciers with gigantic grottos beneath them – some even accessible *(www.nord landsnaturen.no)*. Knut Hamsun's country is the north of the *fylke* between Bodø and Narvik: a paradise on the coast. Offshore lie the Lofoten Islands – they are so unique that there is a special chapter devoted to them in this guide.

People who visit a Nordland island far out at sea are always given a warm welcome and can take an active part in the daily lives of the fishermen and fish farmers.

Beneath the clouds: time flies by in the Norwegian Aviation Museum

BODØ

(136 B4) *(⌂ F8)* **Sharp tongues claim that it is always windy in Bodø (pop. 36,500) and actually the harbour town and Nordland's capital lies open to Vestfjord.**

Only the 800 m (2600 ft) high rugged peaks on Landego Island off the coast provide a little protection from the icy storms from the north west.

Bodø received its town charter in 1860 but the German attack on 27 May 1940 destroyed the entire built-up area. That is why, today, many visitors think Bodø seems rather boring; there are not many buildings or residential areas worth seeing. But the people living in Bodø make up for that: when you take a stroll over the Moloveien on the seashore you will soon recognise that the Bodøværinger are warm-hearted and open-minded – their good humour typifies the town.

Bodø is also major a traffic junction. This is the terminus of the Nordland railway and the Hurtigruten ships dock directly opposite the station. This is where many holiday-makers take a ferry to the Lofoten. Express ships set off for the remote regions and islands on both sides of Vestfjord. This is also the nursery of the Northern-Atlantic cod and if you want to eat a delicious dish of this fish, Bodø is the right place to do so.

SIGHTSEEING

BODIN KIRKE

The stone church, built around 1240, lies directly on Saltfjord about 3 km from the town centre. The richly decorated altar-piece from 1670 is especially noteworthy. *Mid-June–end of Aug Mon–Fri 10am–3pm*

KEISERVARDEN ✲

An easy, three-hour hike over the nearby hills will be rewarded with the most beautiful view over the North Sea to the Lofoten Wall. From 350 m (1150 ft) up, just below the treeline, you can watch the midnight sun sink until it barely touches the sea before rising again – provided that the weather is fine. Concerts are also held here during the *Nordland Music Festival*. More information and hiking maps are available at the Tourist Information Office

NORSK LUFTFARTSMUSEUM

The history of Norwegian civil aviation and the air force, a flight simulator and the depiction of what happens when a plane takes off or lands: exciting impressions for young and old. *Mid-June–mid-Aug daily 10am–6pm, at other times Mon–Fri 10am–4pm, Sat/Sun 11am–5pm | entrance fee 95 NOK | www.luftfart.museum.no*

NYHOLMEN KULTURHISTORISK OMRÅDE (LIGHTHOUSE AND ENTRENCHMENT) ⚓

The reconstructed entrenchment that protected the trading station at Hundholmen, the later town of Bodø, between 1810 and 1835 is located on a small island just offshore from the town. If you walk to the lighthouse, you will have a fine view of Bodø and the surrounding area from the sea.

INSIDER TIP SALTEN MUSEUM – NORDLANDSMUSEET BODØ

The everyday life of Nordland's fish farmers and the Sami settlements are the main subjects in the oldest building in Nordland (built in 1903). Bodø's iron-age silver treasure, which was found in 1919, is also kept here. *May–Aug daily 9am–4pm, Sat/Sun 11am–4pm, at other times Mon–Fri 9am–3pm | entrance fee 35 NOK | Prinsensgate 116 | www.saltenmuseum.no*

FOOD & DRINK

INSIDER TIP FARMORS STUE ● ⏲

A delightfully cosy atmosphere with white tablecloths and the smell of coffee is to be found in 'Grandma's Room'. The snacks and cakes are made using organic ingredients. *Kongens gate 27 | tel. 75 52 78 60 | www.farmorsstue.no | Budget–Moderate*

LØVOLDS KAFETERIA

This is where you can get reasonably-priced Norwegian home-style cooking. The restaurant swears by products from the Arctic. *Tollbugta 9 | tel. 75 52 02 61 | cafeteria.lovold.wips.no | Budget*

SHOPPING

Seeing that it is always windy and sometimes quite cold, an entire street of shops in Bodø has been glazed over: you will find everything you need in the *Glashuset* in the centre. Souvenirs, jewellery and useful articles made of (mostly local) stone, can be bought at *Bertnes Geo-Senter (www.bertnesgeosenter.no | around 8 km (5 mi) east of Bodø).*

SPORTS & ACTIVITIES

FISHING

Fishing is possible everywhere here. In the fjord and on the open sea, from the shore or a boat. Salmon, cod and halibut of

---

⭐ **Kjerringøy**
Ancient coastal traditions are coming back to life on the peninsula to the north of Bodø → p. 75

⭐ **Saltstraumen**
Unbelievable power: the fastest tidal river in Norway is a terrifyingly beautiful natural phenomenon → p. 76

⭐ **Svartisen**
North Norway's largest glacier reaches down to the sea, protects the hinterland from storms and conceals many secrets within it → p. 76

MARCO POLO HIGHLIGHTS

BODØ

Trade and change in Northern Norway: Kjerringøy tells about merchant life in times gone by

seemingly record size can be caught on the *cutter trips on the Saltstraumen*. The size of the boat, length of the excursion and price vary according to the number of people taking part. *Info: Tuvsjyen AS | tel. 75 58 77 91 | www.tuvsjyen.com*

INSIDER TIP NORDLANDSBADET ●

One of the loveliest water parks in Norway and a place where you can pamper yourself. In addition to the various swimming pools and slides, there are whirlpools and corners where you can relax – and a spa area with grottos, various temperature zones, a herbal steam bath and Finnish sauna on the first floor. *Mon–Fri 10am–2am, Sat/Sun 10am–6pm | entrance fee 120 (weekends 140) NOK | spa area Mon–Fri noon–9pm, Sat to 8pm, Sun to 6pm (entrance fee 200/230 NOK) | Plassmyrveien | www.bodospektrum.no*

SEA EAGLE SAFARI

The morning *Sea Eagle Safari* to *Landego* is really exciting and finishes up with a substantial lunch. Further information from the Tourist Information Office only.

WHERE TO STAY

It is worthwhile passing by the Tourist Information Office before choosing where to spend the night. They have a daily listing of where reasonably-priced rooms are available.

SALTSTRAUMEN HOTEL & CAMPING

This idyllic hotel lies 35 km (21¾mi) from Bodø on Road 17 in the midst of wonderful scenery directly on the tidal River Saltstraumen. Cosy cabins and good Norwegian cooking. Spa facilities include a sauna and bathtubs outside in the fresh air. *28 rooms, 12 cabins | Saltstraumen | tel. 75 50 65 00 | www.satstraumenhotell.no | Moderate*

SKAGEN HOTEL

This hotel, where the breakfast chef conjures up delicious dishes requested by the guests and keeps everybody happy, is tastefully decorated and – in spite of its central location – very peaceful. *71 rooms | Nyholmsgata 11 | tel. 75 51 91 00 | www.skagen-hotel.no | Expensive*

INFORMATION

Turistinformasjon | Sentrumsterminalen | tel. 75 54 80 00 | www.visitbodo.com

WHERE TO GO

KJERRINGØY ★ (136 C4) *(⏷ F7)*
Traditional trading centre with 15 buildings from the 19th century in an absolutely beautiful coastal setting. Here you will get a good impression of the everyday life led by the masters and their servants in a typical Norwegian merchant town in times gone by – and you'll feel that a lot is familiar if you have read Knut Hamsun's novels *(end of May–end of Aug daily 11am–5pm | entrance fee 70 NOK, tour 40 NOK | www.saltenmuseum.no)*. The INSIDER TIP *Markens Grøde Café (end of July–end of Aug)* only uses products from neighbouring Kjerringøy organic farm. A hike from the Kjerringøy parsonage to ☊ *Middagshaugen* mountain is worthwhile (don't forget to put on your hiking boots). *38 km (24 mi) north of Bodø on Road 834*

RØST AND VÆRØY (136 A4) *(⏷ E7)*
You can reach these bird islands either in the 35-seat plane operated by Widerøe or by ferry from Bodø. The approximately 1400 people who have their home on these islands live from fish. The constant wind, mild winters and cool summers make it the perfect place for producing dried cod that is then exported to southern Europe. The cliffs on the south-west of the island provide shelter for gigantic colonies of seabirds. A quarter of Norway's entire seabird population nests on the rocks of Røst – and that means around 2.5 million birds: puffins, gulls, cormorants

THE ENDLESS COAST

A magic word all over Norway: since 1893, the ● *Hurtigruten* ships have plied their way between Bergen and Kirkenes. The 4600 km (2875 mi) return voyage takes 11 days and that means that 11 ships are also needed. The route mainly crosses peaceful waters between the skerries and islands. Tourists are especially fond of tours on Hurtigruten ships between April and October but there is a lot to discover on the Norwegian coast from the sea at any time of the year. It is a good idea to choose the off-season, seeing that the trip alone – excluding flight, insurance, etc. – can costs anything from around £750 to more than £11,000 per person. *Information and booking: www. hurtigruten.co.uk/norway*

and sea eagles. The tourist offices on the islands can give further information on boat trips to the bird rocks. *Røst is 100 km (63 mi) from Bodø (the ferry takes around 7 hours) Værøy 85 km (54 mi) (around 4.5 hours)*

The Saltstraumen is Norway's most powerful tidal river

SALTSTRAUMEN ★ (136 B4) (*F8*)
The most savage tidal river in the country is even a gruesomely beautiful sight from far away. Within a mere 6 hours, masses of water are forced through the 3 km (1.9 mi) long and only 150 m wide sound at almost 40 km/h – you can even hear the thundering of the force of nature from the bridge. Fishermen appreciate other qualities that this fjord entrance has to offer: this is where the largest rock salmon in Europe are caught, the record is 22.7 kg (50 lb). If you want to experience the force of the current at close quarters you can sign up for a rafting tour. *(Saltstraumen Naturopplevelser | tel. 99 42 76 06 | info@saltstraumen-adventure.com). 33 km (20½mi) east of Bodø*

SULITJELMA (136 C4) (*F8*)
The former mining town of Sulitjelma where copper was extracted between 1887 and 1991, lies at the end of Road 830, surrounded by threatening mountain ranges and glaciers. The difference in altitude in the galleries of the mines is more than 1200 m (almost 4000 ft) but the *pit railway (end of June–mid-Aug daily 11am–5pm | 200 NOK)* only goes 1500 m into the heart of the mountain The *Mining Museum (in summer, daily 11am–5pm | entrance fee 35 NOK)* 1000 m away gives an overview of 100 years of mining. *www.saltenmuseum.no | 106 km (66 mi) to the east*

SVARTISEN ★ (136 B5) (*E–F 8–9*)
You can get very close to Norway's second largest glacier if you approach it from the sea. *Engabreen*, a glacier snout that reaches down to the shore, is an especially popular tourist destination. In summer, small ships depart daily from the village of *Holand* (170 km/106 mi from Bodø) for the glacier; visitors have to cover the last 1000 metres to the *Cafe Svartispaviljonen*, with a magnificent view of the mighty main glacier, on foot or by bus. If you want to, you can walk a further 2 km until you reach the ice. *(Glacier hikes May–Oct | info and bookings at Rocks 'n*

Rivers | tel. 41 08 29 81 | 800 NOK for 4½ hours). www.rocksnrivers.no

INSIDER TIP ▶ TRÆNA

(136 A5) (Ⓜ E9)

There are good reasons for visiting Norway's smallest community (pop. 464). Only three of the almost 1000 islands and islets near the Arctic Circle are inhabited, and the people here have all grown up with the sea. They are fishermen or involved in salmon farming and happy to see any visitor who comes by. Even hobby anglers will be very successful in the fishing grounds between the islands, and the enormous puffin colony on the island of *Lovund* is a fascinating spectacle. At the beginning of July, the *Træna Festival (3-day pass 90 NOK | www.trena.net)* takes place: first-rate rock and pop from Norway, around 2000 – mostly young – visitors, tent camps, fine seafood straight off the cutter, sun and rain are the ingredients that make this an unforgettable experience at the Arctic Circle. Accommodation is available in the *Træna Rorbuferie* fishing huts *(tel. 75 09 53 80 | www.rorbu-ferie.com | Budget)* on Husøy. *www.trana.kommune. no | 140 km (88 mi) from Bodø | express ship from Bodø or Sandnessjøen/Nesna/ Stokkvågen (same ship)*

NARVIK

(137 D3) (Ⓜ G6) **Some of the fiercest battles in World War II were fought in Narvik (pop. 14,000). The reason was the harbour's economic and strategic importance.**

Iron ore from the mines in Kiruna in Sweden is still shipped out of Narvik today. The gigantic loading wharfs are the first and most dominating, impression of

BOOKS & FILMS

▶ **Out Stealing Horses** – This novel by Per Petterson has won many international awards and deals with universal problems: confronting the past and the truth.

▶ **Don't Look Back** – Karin Fossum made her literary debut in Norway in 1974. The author of crime fiction, often referred to as the 'Norwegian queen of crime', also writes poetry and short stories. It is with her Inspector Sejer mysteries that Fossum has won greatest acclaim and the series has been published in 16 languages. Other successful titles include 'Calling Out For You'; her most recent works are 'Bad Intentions and The Caller'.

▶ **Kitchen Stories** – Director Bent Hamer has made it to Hollywood. His first film 'Eggs' (1995) was followed by the prize-winning 'Kitchen Stories' in 2003 – a somewhat off-beat story with gentle humour, little dialogue and first-class character performances.

▶ **Trollhunter** – Anybody who believed that there were no trolls in Norway was shown that this is not true in this film (2011), directed by André Øvredal. During the day, the gnarled giants are not dangerous but at night they have been know to flatten a forest or steal a sheep from the meadow. This parody on documentary films can make you shudder a little – and laugh a lot.

a town that is located in a magnificent setting.

SIGHTSEEING

FJELLHEISEN (CABLE CAR) ☼

If you decide to stay in town but still want to have a fine view, the cable car *(fjellheisen)* can be recommended – it will whisk you up to an altitude of 656 m (2100 ft) in a mere seven minutes. When the sky is blue, the fjord and fjell – and sometimes the midnight sun – combine to create a breathtaking panorama. *In summer daily noon–1am*

NORDLAND RØDE KORS KRIGSMINNENMUSEUM

The battles for Narvik and its iron ore as well as the destruction of the town in World War II are recorded this museum. The exhibition is well worth seeing and thought provoking. *In summer Mon–Sat 10am–9pm, Sun noon–6pm | entrance fee 50 NOK | an the Market Square | www. fred.no*

INSIDER TIP OFOTBANEN ☼

The Ofot Railway, one of the most exciting stretches of track in Europe, runs between fjords and Arctic plateaus. Travelling on this train will give you an idea of the hardships the migrant workers who built the line more than 100 years ago had to endure. The return trip to the Swedish border *(Riksgränsen)* costs 180 NOK. *Daily 10.30am, return around 4pm | tickets at the ticket machines in Narvik*

FOOD & DRINK

ROYAL BLUE

The fresh charr is one of the most delicious of the North-Norwegian specialities served in this exclusive restaurant in the Grand Royal Hotel. *Kongensgate 64 | tel. 76 97 70 00 | info.q.royal@choice.no | Expensive*

SPORTS & ACTIVITIES

Alpine sports are very popular between the fjord and fjell: World Cup races are even held in Narvik. The cable cars and lifts are in operation until late May. The ski centre is in the middle of town making distances between your accommodation and the slopes short. Narvik after a

---

LOW BUDGET

▶ Island-hopping by bicycle will make it easy for you to discover the island and skerry paradise along Helgeland's coast and also bring you closer to the culture and people. Tips for routes and maps can be obtained from the tourist information offices. *125 NOK per day (incl. helmet) | tel. 75 01 80 00 | www. visithelgeland.com*

▶ The fjell farm *Furuheim Gård* in Susendal provides fresh produce straight from the field, overnight stays in untamed natural surroundings, culture and plenty of other activities. *Overnight stay 300 NOK per person, breakfast and supper 50 NOK per meal | Hattfjeelldal | tel. 75 18 56 23 | www.furuheimgaard.no*

▶ Enjoy health food: The ☺ *Helgeland Matfestival*, the largest organic foods festival in Norway, is the place to go to taste and enjoy unusual, as well as traditional, culinary delights. All this along with good entertainment, music and cooking competitions. *17–19 Aug | entrance fee 40 NOK | Mosjøen | www. helgelandmatfestival.no*

fresh snowfall is a top address among snowboarders.

WHERE TO STAY

NORDSTJERNEN HOTELL
A reasonably priced hotel of a simple standard. In winter, many young skiers stay here. Those seeking peace and quiet are best advised to stay here in the summer only. *25 rooms | Kongensgate 26 | tel. 76 94 41 20 | www.nordstjernen.no | Moderate*

NORUMGÅRDEN BED & BREAKFAST
Magnificent wooden villa in a suburb a bit out of the centre; decorated with antiques and beautifully furnished rooms. *4 rooms | Framnesvei 127 | tel. 76 94 48 57 | norum gaarden.narviknett.no | Budget*

INFORMATION

Turistinformasjon | Destination Narvik | Kongensgate 57 | tel. 76 96 56 00 | www. destinationnarvik.com

WHERE TO GO

HAMARØY (136 C3) *(Ø F7)*
'The sky all open and clean; I stared into that clear sea, ...'. This sentence in Knut Hamsun's book *Pan* was written during the many years he spent on the Hamarøy Peninsula. The community lies in a picturesque coastal setting among bizarre peaks. The Hamsunsenter *(mid-June– mid-Aug daily 11am–6pm, shorter opening hours at other times | entrance fee 70 NOK | Presteid | www.hamsunsenteret.no)* created by the American architect Steven Holl shows the most comprehensive exhibition on the life and work of the famous novelist anywhere. There is also a very special place to spend the night on Hamarøy: in the lighthouse *Tranøy fyr (13 rooms | tel. 91 32 80 13 | www.tranoyfyr.no | Moderate)* you will fall asleep with the tang of salt on your lips and the shriek of seagulls in your ears. This is also a place where anglers will be able to reel in some impressive cod. *100 km (62 mi) south of Narvik*

Endless views in the far north: Tranøy fyr lighthouse on the Hamarøy peninsula

LOFOTEN

Even getting there is an experience: no matter whether you come by ferry or plane from the mainland: the massive Lofoten Wall will immediately hit your eye rising up out of Vestfjord.

Many fishing villages lie between these peaks and the arable land; small towns and historical treasure troves are hidden in the hinterland. The Lofoten archipelago stretches 150 km (93 mi) northwards along the west side of Vestfjord.

The car ferry departs from Bodø for Mosekenes *(around 3½ hours)* or from Skutvik for Svolvær *(2 hours)*. You can reach Svolvær by catamaran from Bodø *(departures Mon–Thu and Sat 5.15pm, Fri 6pm, Sun 8pm | travel time around 3 hours | no cars | ruteinfo.ovds.no).*

The 'overland route', with many bridges and a short ferry crossing, is the E10 from Narvik as far as Å, the southernmost point of the island group directly next to the Moskenes ferry wharf – a trip that takes in all of the main islands of the Lofoten. Anybody who visits the Lofoten should spend at least one night in a *rorbu*. For almost 1000 years, these houses built on piles in the water were where the fishermen lived during the fishing season. The modern versions are robust and equipped completely differently (booking at Destination Lofoten in Svolvær).

Photo: Sakrisøy

Alpine peaks and the depths of the ocean: fishing is important, but it is mainly tourism that breathes life into this group of islands

LEKNES

(136 B3) *(ʃ E7)* **As is the case with all of the other larger towns on the Lofoten, Leknes (pop. 2600) is not especially attractive.**

Leknes is the centre of the island and community of Vestvågøy and has an important airport. The post-war architecture has no charm at all but the surroundings of the small town have a lot to offer.

SIGHTSEEING

LOFOTR VIKING MUSEUM IN BORG ★
This is how the predecessors of the Norwegians lived: this museum is located to the north of Leknes and is an impressive reconstruction of the largest house

REINE

Nusfjord, a picture-postcard Lofoten harbour

from the Viking period ever found (83 m/ 272 ft long). The Vikings held political and religious meetings in the 'guildhall' of the house. *June–Aug daily 10am–7pm, shorter opening hours at other times | entrance fee 120 NOK | www.lofotr.no*

FOOD & DRINK

SKJÆBRYGGA

Excellent fish dishes are served here directly on the quay. The restaurant is in Stamsund, 15 km (9¼ mi) to the east of

Leknes. *Tel. 76 05 46 00 | www.skjaebrygga. no | Moderate*

SHOPPING

Drive around 15 km (9 mi) south of Leknes and then turn to the right towards the North Sea. There you will find the village of Vikten with Åse and Åsvar Tangrand's glass blowing and pottery workshop. The two artists give their imagination free rein – much to the delight of the visitors who make the effort to come here. *June– Aug daily 10am–7pm | entrance to the workshop and 'Potter's Tower' 20 NOK*

WHERE TO STAY

STORFJORD CAMPING OG HYTTER

In a fairy-tale setting on Vestfjord. In Steine, around 20 km (12.5 mi) east of Leknes (turn off Road 817 near Storfjord). *10 cabins | tel. 76 08 68 04 | post@storfjord camping.no | Budget*

INFORMATION

Destination Lofoten | Torget Svolvær | tel. 76 06 98 07 | www.lofoten.info

REINE

(136 B3) (*ll E7*) ⚓ Reine is picturesque in the true sense of the word. Generations of landscape painters and photographers have come to the main town on the southern-most Lofoten island Moskenes (pop. 1400) to capture their impressions of the contrasts in the scenery that range from pointed mountain peaks to pretty villages and clear water.

There is the smell of fish drying on the racks typical of the Lofoten everywhere here from March to autumn. Some of the most beautiful viewpoints and fishing villages in the Lofoten are in this area.

SIGHTSEEING

FLAKSTAD KIRKE ★
The church, a red log cabin built entirely of lost cargo was washed ashore from ships, lies around 30 km (19 mi) south of Reine on the E10 just before Ramberg. Its magnificent location makes it one of the most impressive houses of worship in Scandinavia.

INSIDER TIP ▶ LOFOTEN TØRRFISKMUSEUM
Å is a living museum village. The production of dried fish has a long tradition on the Lofoten and that is shown here in the buildings of a traditional fish factory. *End of June–end of Aug daily 11am–5pm, at other times, by appointment | entrance fee 40 NOK | at the end of the E10*

MOSKENESSTRAUMEN
The strait lies between the southern tip of the Lofoten, Lofotodden, and the island of Værøy. There are guided walks to the legendary maelstrom, made famous by Edgar Allan Poe, in summer.

NUSFJORD
The fishing village on the Vestfjord has been a Unesco World Heritage site since 1975. Most of the *rorbus* date from the 19th century and have been restored and turned into holiday accommodation. *www.nusfjord.no | south on the E10, turn left after Kilan*

SAKRISØY
The more than 100-year-old, ochre-coloured huts in this fishing settlement form a fantastic contrast to the surrounding mountains. Where to stay: *Buene på Valen | tel. 90 06 15 66 | www.sakrisoy.no/*

buene.htm | *Moderate* | *3.5 km (2 mi) north on the E10*

FOOD & DRINK

RAMBERG GJESTEGÅRD
Here you will be served Lofoten Island lamb as well as fish and even whale meat. There is also a beach of fine sand and ten dwellings. *Ramberg | tel. 76 09 35 00 | www.ramberg-gjestegard.no | Moderate*

SPORTS & ACTIVITIES

Bicycles and boats are available for rent at almost all places to stay. You can fish from the shore or from a boat.

WHERE TO STAY

MAREN ANNA
This guesthouse in Sørvågen lies directly on the water, the rooms with a view are cosy and bright, the speciality of the restaurant is rock salmon roasted with lemon. *12 rooms | tel. 76 09 20 50 | www.lofoten-info.no/marenanna | Budget*

★ **Lofotr Viking Museum in Borg**
The way the forefathers of the Norwegians lived: a replica of an 83-metre-long house from Viking times has been built on the island of Vestvågøy → p. 81

★ **Flakstad Kirke**
The dazzlingly red church is the most beautiful house of worship on the Lofoten → p. 82

★ **Trollfjord**
A fairy-tale fjord arm – and so narrow that big ships can hardly turn around → p. 84

MARCO POLO HIGHLIGHTS

Drying fish in the fresh air has a long tradition on the Lofoten

INFORMATION

Turistkontoret Flakstad & Moskenes | Moskenes ferry wharf | tel. 98 01 75 64 | tour-ff@lofoten-info.no

SVOLVÆR

(136 B3) (Ⅲ F7) The capital of the Lofoten lies beneath the Svolvægeita Mountain (Solvær Goat); it has this name because its two peaks resemble horns.
The value of the landed cod, herrings and farmed salmon makes Solvær (pop. 4100) one of the most important fishing ports in North Norway. The racks used for drying fish around the town centre, which can also be seen on the smaller islands, are clear evidence of this.

SIGHTSEEING

LOFOTMUSEET
The regional museum was established on the remains of Vågar, the only town in North Norway in the Middle Ages. The main building is a grand merchant's house from 1815; the everyday life of simple people is the main focus of the exhibition in the other houses. And, of course, fishing and cargo boats make up most of the exhibits. The 2 km (1¼ mi) long path, 'The First Town in the North', leads you to seven cultural monuments. *In summer daily 10am–6pm, shorter opening hours at other times | entrance 60 NOK | Storvågen (section of Kabelvåg) | www.lofotmuseet.no*

TROLLFJORD ★
Large tourist ships have to turn around in this extremely narrow side-arm of Raftsund. While this is happening, passengers admire the rocky shore rising straight up to the skies and the fascinating play of light on the water. *June–Aug several trips on the fjord (2½–4 hours) | tickets from Destination Lofoten*

FOOD & DRINK

BØRSEN SPISERI/SVINØYA RORBUER
The maritime restaurant Børsen Spiseri (reservation advisable) is associated with

the 30 *rorbus* that can accommodate two to six guests. *Gunnars Vergs vei 4 | tel. 76 06 99 30 | www.svinoya.no | Moderate*

SHOPPING

SKANDINAVISK HØYFJELLSUTSTYR

In case you forget something you need for your outward-bound holiday: the experts in this shop not only know everything about the land and water in the vicinity, they can also provide you with the all the necessary equipment. *Håkon Kyllingsmarks gate 3*

SPORTS & ACTIVITIES

ANGLING

In summer, cutters and tourist ships take hobby anglers out to sea. Anybody who wants to, can participate in the *World Cod Fishing Championship* at the end of March. *More information from Destination Lofoten*

BICYCLE TOURS

Starting in Svolvær through the countryside of the northern Lofoten: the 220-km-long (136 mi) INSIDER TIP *Kaiser Route*, one of Europe's most magnificent bike tours, will take you to remote places that are hardly ever reached by car – along Raftsund with world-famous Trollfjord and back to the start. Cycling is most enjoyable in the evening. If you are lucky, harbour porpoises or even killer whales will accompany on your way through Raftsund. *www. lofoten.info/article.php?id=630*

INSIDER TIP RAFTING ☙

Even if the weather is fine and there are no waves, the currents and views will make discovering the Lofoten from an inflatable raft an exciting experience. There are regular tours in summer (inquire by phone) and killer whale safaris from October to January. Appropriate clothing is provided.

From 400 NOK | Lofoten Seafari | tel. 41 47 00 00 | www.lofoten-seafari.no

WHERE TO STAY

RICA HOTEL SVOLVÆR

This modern hotel lies in perfect harmony with nature on a small island in the harbour. *146 rooms | tel. 76 07 22 22 | www.rica.no | Expensive*

SVOLVÆR SJØHUSCAMPING

The atmosphere in this house on the quay only a few minutes from the centre of town is rustically maritime and cosy. Rooms with two or four beds, as well as a holiday flat, are available. *13 rooms | Parkgata 12 | tel. 76 07 03 36 | www.svolver-sjohus camping.no | Budget*

INFORMATION

Destination Lofoten | Torget | tel. 76 06 98 00 | www.lofoten.info

LOW BUDGET

▶ The *Munkebu Hut* lies in the Djupfjordheia highlands not far from Sørvågen, and *Selfjordhytta* on the picturesque Selfjord near Flakstad. Take your own sheets and food with you! Many hiking possibilities. *15 beds in each | 250 NOK per person | www.turist foreningen.no | www.lofoten-turlag.no*

▶ *Vikingmarked:* Viking Day at the Viking Centre in Borg offers handicrafts, games and music just like 1000 years ago, as well as interesting talks. The entrance is free! *8–12 Aug | www.lofotr.no*

TROMS

Welcome to Arctic Europe. The treeline sinks lower all the time and the mountain ranges towering out of the ocean become increasingly barren.

There is jewel-like scenery at the foot of the mountains, sandy beaches and old fishing villages on the islands, and rivers full of fish and broad valleys in the interior. However, you will only be able to enjoy the stable summer weather protected by a mosquito net. Tourism on Svalbard profits from the natural scenery of the Arctic and the history of the island group as a whaling and sealing station. Large areas are protected and outdoor activities strictly regulated. The 'Land of the Pointed Mountains', as it was called by its discoverer Willem Barents in 1596, cannot sustain mass tourism.

SVALBARD (SPITS-BERGEN)

(134 A–B 1–2) (𝄞 N–01) ★ Ice-capped mountains with glaciers on their slopes running into the sea, high mountain valleys that are only free of snow in the west and at the height of summer; but, the 'Land of the Cold Coasts' is not an icy desert

Photo: Tromsø

Cold coastal area and green islands:
the great expanse of the north from Tromsø
to the 'Land of the Pointed Mountains'

A side arm of the Golf Stream is to be thanked for it never becoming really cold on the west side of Spitsbergen, the inhabited main island in Svalbard: the average temperature in summer is 6°C (43°F) and minus 12°C (+10°F) in winter. The summer is made even more pleasant by the midnight sun: it never becomes really dark between 19 April and 22 August. Around 3700 people live on Svalbard, around one third of them in the main town Longyearbyen and smaller settlements.

FOOD & DRINK

FRUENE KAFFE & VINBAR
This is where you can get fresh bread and pastries, lunches and various types of coffee. *Lompensenteret | tel. 79 02 76 40*

The Polarmuseet on the harbour in Tromsø will take you on an expedition to the Arctic Ocean

WHERE TO STAY

INSIDER TIP **SPITSBERGEN GUESTHOUSE**

Today, you can find reasonably-priced accommodation where the workers in the coalmine used to live – on the outskirts of town and below the mountains and glaciers. Meals are still served in the 'main mess hall' that is a meeting place for guests from all over the world with one thing in common: they all want to discover Svalbard. *75 rooms | tel. 79 02 63 00 | www.spitsbergentravel.no | Budget*

SPITSBERGEN HOTEL ☼

This was also once used for housing by the coal-mining company. It is now a great place to relax in cosy surroundings. *88 rooms | tel. 79 02 62 00 | www.spits bergentravel.no | Expensive*

INFORMATION

Svalbard Reiseliv | Longyearbyen | tel. 79 02 55 50 | www.svalbard.net

TROMSØ

(137 D1) (⌀ G5) ★ The most northerly university city in the world has no lack of superlatives: with 2558m² Tromsø is the largest city in Norway in terms of area, it is the most densely populated city north of the Arctic Circle (pop. 55,000) and the city with the lowest average age.

And, in relation to the population, nowhere else are there as many hotels, restaurants and pubs as in the 'Paris of the North'. Sometimes it happens that there is still snow on the ground when the midnight sun, which shines here from 23 May to 23 July, makes its first appearance. But this is still reason enough for people to sit outside until late in the evening.

SIGHTSEEING

FJELLHEISEN (CABLE CAR) ☼

The trip to the *Storsteinen* mountain view point (421 m/1380m ft) can be especially recommended on a summer evening. A refreshing drink under the midnight sun – it's all possible here! *20 May–20 Aug daily 10am–1am | cable car 99 NOK*

ISHAVSKATEDRALEN

The church is really called Tromsdalen Kirke. But, shortly after its consecration in 1965 it was renamed the 'Arctic Ocean Cathedral' because the large, aluminium-coated concrete panels and triangular form created associations with an iceberg. The gigantic glass mosaic on the east wall is especially impressive as are the *Midnight Sun Concerts* (regularly in summer, programme from the Tourist Information Office). *In summer Mon–Sat 9am–7pm, Sun 1–7pm, at other times daily 4–6pm | entrance fee 50 NOK | www.ishavskatedralen.no*

MACKS ØLBRYGGERI

A visit to the northern-most brewery in the world is topped off by half a litre of your choice in the beer hall. *Tours Mon–Thu 1pm | entrance fee 150 NOK | www.mack.no*

POLARMUSEET

Norway's polar history, expeditions and seal and polar bear hunting are the themes in the Polar Museum that has been set up between the old harbour warehouses. *In summer daily 10am–7pm, shorter opening hours at other times | entrance fee 60 NOK | www.polarmuseum.no*

TROMSØ BRU (TOWN BRIDGE)

The 43 m (141ft) high Tromsø Bridge spans the Tromsøsund and joins the suburb of Tromsdalen with the centre. Walking across it is an absolute must simply for the view.

FOOD & DRINK

ALLEGRO

Pasta and pizza between the Arctic Ocean Cathedral and cable car. *Turistveien 19 | tel. 77 68 80 71 | Budget*

SKARVEN

The perfect place for a *helaften* – a long, pleasant evening. It can begin in the *Biffhuset (Moderate)* steak restaurant on the first floor or higher up in the *Arctandria (Expensive)* fish restaurant, continue in the *Kroa (Budget)* pub that is famous throughout Norway, and finish up in the cocktail bar in the basement. *Strandtorget | tel. 77 60 07 20 | www.skarven.no*

SHOPPING

The light of the north really makes itself felt in the artistic products created by the Blåst glass blowing workshop *(Peder Hansensgate 4 | www.blaast.no)*.

ENTERTAINMENT

It is fun to spend the evening in the Storgata pedestrian precinct going from pub to pub and waiting for night to fall – because, this never happens in summer. The ideal place to start is the *Ølhallan*, the 'Beer Hall' *(open until 6pm, closed on Sunday | Storgata 4 | www.olhallen.no)*.

★ **Svalbard (Spitsbergen)**
Norway's arctic outpost
→ p. 86

★ **Tromsø**
Nobody wants to go to bed here in summer → p. 88

★ **Lyngsalpen**
Paradise under the midnight sun for climbers → p. 90

★ **Andenes**
Sandy beaches, the North Sea and enormous sperm whales → p. 91

MARCO POLO HIGHLIGHTS

WHERE TO STAY

ABC HOTELL NORD
Small, simple hotel in quiet surroundings. *22 rooms | Parkgata 4 | tel. 77 66 83 00 | www.hotellnord.no | Budget*

RICA ISHAVSHOTEL
Its location and ship shape make it impossible not to notice this hotel. The rooms are modern but some of them have carpets in very strong colours. If you don't like this, ask for a room *uten gulvbelleg* (without a carpet) but *med utsikt* (with a view). *180 rooms | Frederik Langesgat 2 (on the sound) | tel. 77 66 64 00 | www.rica.no | Expensive*

INFORMATION

Destinasjon Tromsø | Kirkegata 2 | tel. 77 61 00 00 | www.destinasjontromso.no

WHERE TO GO

LYNGSALPEN ⭐ (137 E1) (*ⅅ H5*)
Lyngseidet is an ideal starting point for exploring the arctic alpine scenery with its, partly ice-covered, peaks reaching up to an altitude of 1800 m (5900 ft). The first mountaineers came here in the middle of the 19th century – today, this is a destination for the bravest off-slope skiers. *Lyngseidet* is around 60 km (37.5 mi) to the east of Tromsø and can be reached along the E8 and Road 91 and then the *Breivikeidet–Svensby ferry (crossing: 20 minutes)*.

SOMMARØY (137 D1) (*ⅅ G5*)
The drive on Road 862 from Tromsø along the south coast of the gigantic *Kvaløya* Island towards the west is an excursion into the fertile agricultural region of Troms and to the beautiful island of Sommarøy. The crystal-clear water, white beaches and flowering front gardens create delightful, colourful contrasts. *80 km (50 mi) west of Tromsø*

INSIDER TIP VOLLAN GJESTESTUE
(137 E1–2) (*ⅅ H5*)
Norway's truck drivers have voted: the best motorway restaurant in the country is where the E6 and E8 meet. The restaurant serves arctic dishes made with the best-quality products from the region. *Nordkjosbotn | tel. 77 72 23 00 | www.vollan-gjestestue.no | 70 km (44 mi) south of Tromsø | Moderate*

LOW BUDGET

▶ *Tromsø Vandrerhjem:* The youth hostel lies in the hills 15 minutes from the town centre. *From 510 NOK for two | tel. 77 65 76 28 | Asgårdveien 9 | tromsohostell@vandrerhjem.no*

▶ 22 self-catering cabins, such as *Senjabu (3 rooms | 35 km (22 mi) from Finnsnes on the island of Senja)* make it possible to enjoy the nature of the fjell and coastal landscape. *250 NOK per person | tel. 77 68 51 75 | www.turistforeningen.no/rooms*

VESTERÅLEN

Part of the Vesterålen island group that continues on from the Lofoten in the north belongs to Nordland, but it is best to discover this area from the north.

One of the ways to do this is by taking the small *ferry (June–Aug 3 departures daily)* from *Gryllefjord* (137 D1) (*ⅅ G5*) (on the west side of Senja Island) to *Andenes*, the northernmost point of the group of islands. Another alternative is to drive on the E10 from *Bjerkvik* (137 D2) (*ⅅ G6*). After

A wave of the fin: organised whale safaris start from the island of Andøya

60 km (37.5 mi), head north to *Harstad* or further to the west to *Sortland* (pop. 4200). Here, you will have to decide whether you want to go on a whale safari to the northern island of *Andøya* or mountain hiking to *Øksnes* (north-west of Sortland).

SIGHTSEEING

ANDENES ⭐

Although surrounded by a wall of mountains and snow-white beaches, the main town on the island of Andøya lies completely at the mercy of the North Sea. Excursions leave the *Whale Centre* for the edge of the Norwegian Shelf where sperm whales regularly show up in summer waiting to be photographed. *End May–mid-Sept daily 9.30am | excursion lasts a good 4 hours | from Andenes harbour | price 830 NOK | bookings necessary | tel. 76 11 56 00 | www.whalesafari.com*

HURTIGRUTEMUSEET STOKMARKNES

Richard With, the 'father' of the Hurtigruten, came from Stokmarknes and that is where the MS Finnmarken has dropped anchor – as a museum. *In summer daily 10am–6pm | entrance fee 90 NOK | 26 km (16 mi) south-west of Sortland on the E10 | www.hurtigrutemuseet.no*

JENNESTAD

One of the many trading posts that were established on the coast of northern Norway in the early 20th century. *Visits and exhibitions in summer Tue–Sun 11am–5pm | entrance fee 30 NOK | 8 km (5 mi) north of Sortland on Road 820*

WHERE TO STAY

HOTEL MARENA

Small, but exquisite. In the centre of Sortland with tastefully decorated rooms. Breakfast with freshly-baked bread is served 70 m away in the stylish but cosy INSIDER TIP *Kafé Steingodt. 21 rooms | Storgata 15 | tel. 91 58 35 17 | www.hotell marena.no | Expensive*

INFORMATION

Vesterålen Reiseliv | Kjøpmannsgata 2 | Sortland | tel. 76 11 14 80 | www.visit vesteralen.com; Andøy Turistinformasjon | Hamnegata 1c | tel. 76 14 12 03 | www. andoyturist.no

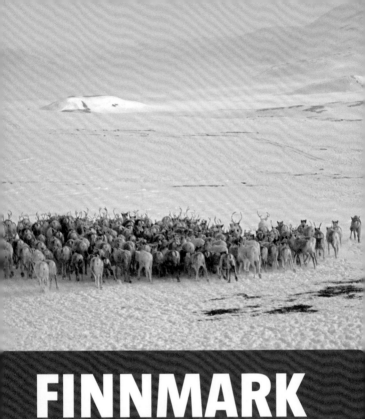

FINNMARK

Icy winds meet open harbours, raging rivers flow into majestic fjords, thousands of peaceful mountain lakes are beleaguered by myriads of mosquitoes.

That is Finnmark: 48,000 m² (18,500 mi²) large and surrounded by the inhospitable coastline of the Arctic Ocean. The interior is characterised by a barren high plateau where tens of thousands of reindeer fight to survive in winter. The 72,500 people who live in Finnmark have a close relationship to nature that, here, shows all of its facets. Temperatures range from 25 degrees above to 50°C below zero (+77° to −58°F). In winter, the houses are battered by storms and in summer people bask in the sun on the beautiful sandy beaches and – from time to time – cool off in the Arctic Ocean; the water can be as warm as 14°C (almost 60°F). In Alta, the midnight sun shines from 16 May to 26 July; and even a few days longer at the North Cape.

ALTA

(138 C3) (∅ K2) **Alta (pop. 13,500) lies on the southern shore of the mighty Altafjord and is the largest town in Finnmark.** The *fylke's* university has been established here and there is also some industry. The Altaelva salmon river flows down from

Photo: Herds of reindeer in Finnmark

The vastness of the Arctic below the North Cape: Barren high plateaus and the Arctic Ocean coastline – Norway's north is full of extremes

Finnmarksvidda through Alta Canyon before flowing into Altafjord.

SIGHTSEEING

ALTA MUSEUM ★

What drove the first people to the northern edge of Europe? What did they live from and what did they believe in? The 3000 rock drawings between 2500 and 6500 years old that were discovered on the western edge of the city give impressive answers to these questions. There is good reason that the Helleristningfelt Hjemmeluft is now one of the Unesco World Heritage Sites. The exhibitions on the prehistory of Finnmark in the Alta Museum are also worth seeing. *End of June–end of Aug daily 8am–8pm shorter opening hours at other times | entrance fee 85 NOK | www.alta-museum.no*

Sami Parliament in Karasjok

price; the actual hike only takes one hour in each direction. *May–mid-Aug daily | bookings at North Adventure | tel. 78 44 50 50 | 800 NOK*

HALDDETOPPEN ☀

The hike to the peak of *Halde Mountain* (904 m/3000 ft) starts near *Kåfjorfd* (20 km/12.5 mi to the west of Alta on the E6). In 1898, the first northern-lights observatory was established here. You should be in good shape if you want to make this climb but you will be rewarded with a magnificent view over Altafjord.

WHERE TO STAY

GARGIA FJELLSTUE

Rustically decorated bedrooms and public areas; guests are welcome to provide their own food and drink. Sami specialities such as *ptarmigan*, charr and cloudberries are served in the restaurant (daily in summer). *11 rooms, 3 cabins | tel. 78 43 33 51 | www.gargia-fjellstue.no | Moderate*

WISLØFF CAMPING

The second of three camp sites 5 km (3 mi) south of Alta is especially spacious. The cabins (for four) are practical, light and attractive. *On the River Alta | tel. 78 43 43 03 | www.wisloeff.no | cabins: Moderate*

INFORMATION

Alta Turistinformasjon | Parksenteret | tel. 78 44 50 50 | www.altatours.no

FOOD & DRINK

INSIDER TIP ALFAOMEGA

The speciality of the house is *Ole Mattis Hætta* – baked smoked reindeer. On weekends, it can become fairly rowdy here but that does not affect the way the food tastes at all! *Markedsgata 14 | tel. 78 44 54 00 | www.alfaomega-alta.no | Moderate*

SPORTS & ACTIVITIES

ALTA CANYON

It is only possible to visit the reservoir and power plant in North Europe's largest canyon on a guided tour. The highlight of the five-hour excursion is lunch on the edge of the ravine. Transport is included in the

HAMMERFEST

(138 C2) (*ΩΩ K1*) **The most northerly city in the world (pop. 6800) has existed since 1789. The incidents in World War II and especially the scorched earth policy of the German occupying forces, mean that**

there are no traces of Hammerfest's former splendour.

The gas from the enormous 'Snow White' field in the Barents Sea is processed in the refinery in Hammerfest and transported all over the world in the form of liquid gas. The off-shore industry has had a lasting effect on the town.

SIGHTSEEING

GJENREISNINGSMUSEET

This museum provides a graphic description of how strongly Hammerfest was affected by World War II and the efforts the Finnmarkingers had to undertake to rebuild it. *In summer Mon–Fri 9am–4pm, Sat/Sun 10am–2pm, at other times 11am–2pm | entrance fee 50 NOK | Kirkegata 21 | www. gjenreisningsmuseet.no*

MERIDIAN COLUMN

This monument was erected in 1854 to commemorate the first survey of the globe that Russia, Sweden and Norway had completed in 1852. *In the Fuglenes district*

FOOD & DRINK

REDRUM CAFÉ & BAR

As is often the case in the north: during the day, a restaurant with good-quality fast food, in the evening a pub and later a live club. An important meeting place. *Storgata 23 | tel. 78 41 00 49 | www.redrum.no | Budget*

WHERE TO STAY

HOTEL SKYTTERHUSET AS

Comparatively reasonably-priced rooms, beautiful location, the comfort is more-or-less average. *75 rooms | Skytterveien 24 | tel. 78 42 20 10 | www.skytterhuset.no | Moderate*

INFORMATION

Turistinformasjon in 'Isbjørnklubben' | Sjøgata 6 | tel. 78 41 21 85 | www.hammer fest-turist.no

KARASJOK

(139 D3) *(ₒ L3)* **The community in the middle of Finnmarksvidda (pop. 2800) is the political centre of Samiland.**
This is the site of the parliament (Sameting) and extensive Sami collections. The town is only 18 km (11 mi) from the Finnish border and this makes it an important junction on the *Nordkalotte* (North Cape).

SIGHTSEEING

KARASJOK GAMLE KIRKE

The Old Church, built in 1807, cam be seen from far away; it is the only building in Karasjok that survived World War II. *In summer, daily 8am–9pm*

⭐ **Alta Museum**
Primeval petroglyphs in a well-designed museum
→ p. 92

⭐ **North Cape**
The midnight sun sinking towards the Arctic Sea but hardly touching it creates an indelible impression
→ p. 97

⭐ **Varanger**
The enormous peninsula in the Arctic Ocean is the epitome of everything that characterises the European Arctic → p. 98

MARCO POLO HIGHLIGHTS

SAMISK KUNSTNERSENTER

Arts and crafts and paintings by Sami artists. *Mon–Fri 10am–4pm, Sat/Sun 1–4pm | entrance free | www.samiskkunstner senter.no*

BOBLE GLASHYTTE

The northern-most glassworks on earth. The everyday objects are characterised by their simplicity and subdued colours while the artworks created by the owner have much more daring shapes and colours. *Sápmi-Park | www.bobleglass.no*

WHERE TO STAY

ENGHOLM HUSKY & VANDRERHJEM

Surrounded by forest, sledge dogs and friendly people. Absolutely recommendable: the summer camps in the vastness of Finnmarksvidda (daily excursions or overnight stays). *15 beds | tel. 78 46 71 66 | www.engholm.no | Budget*

INFORMATION

Sapmi KS | Porsangerveien 1 | tel. 78 46 88 00 | www.sapmi.no

KAUTOKEINO

(138 C4) (m K3) Kautokeino (pop. almost 3000), the Sami's capital, lies around 130 km (80 mi) south of Alta.
Kautokeino has a Sami theatre, Sami university and the Sami major festival is held at Easter *(www.samieasterfestival.com)*

SIGHTSEEING

JUHLS' SILVER GALLERY

This silversmith workshop is the life's works of two artists who have united Sami traditions with modern art and attempted to transmit their impressions of the landscapes, myths and people in Finnmark. *In summer daily 9am–8pm, at other times 9am–6pm | free tours | www.juhls.no*

PIKEFOSSEN

45 km (28 mi) to the north of Kautokeino and Road 93, this magnificent waterfall plummets down towards Alta. There is a rest area directly on the road and it is also possible to camp near the river.

FOOD & DRINK

KAUTOKEINO VILLMARKSENTER AS

This guesthouse is run by Sami who serve their traditional dishes. Weary guests can also stay overnight in a room or cabin (32 beds). In summer, tourist information office. *Tel 78 48 76 02 | www.mamut.com/vmsenter | Moderate*

INFORMATION

Turistinformasjon | tel. 95 75 51 99 | www.kautokeino.nu

NORTH CAPE

(139 D1) *(ΩΩ L1)* ⭐ **This is not the northernmost point but still an unforgettable experience. The 307 m (1017 ft) high plateau on the island of Magerøy is 2163 km (1350 mi) from Oslo.**

You reach the island through a 6.8 km (4¼ mi) long tunnel *(toll: up to a total length of 6 m; 145 NOK plus 47 NOK per passenger, in each direction)*. There are restaurants, souvenirs, a panorama bar and a small ecumenical chapel in the gigantic North Cape Hall. But the real drama at latitude 71°10′21″ north is performed on the northern horizon if no fog or cloud veils the midnight sun. *www.nordkapp.no*

SIGHTSEEING

KIRKEPORTEN ☼

The hike to the 'church door' rock is not very strenuous. From here, you have a fabulous view over the North Sea and towards the North Cape. *Starting point: near Kirkeporten Camping in Skarsvåg*

INSIDER TIP GJESVÆRSTAPPAN

You should try to get a close-up view of the spectacle taking place on this bird rock: cormorants, puffins, seagulls and sea eagles. *Gjesvær Turistsenter | tel. 41 61 39 83 | www.birdsafari.com (in summer, three tours daily | 500 NOK per person); Roald Berg | Gjesvær | tel. 95 03 77 22 | www.stappan.no | tours daily | 500 NOK)*

WHERE TO STAY

INSIDER TIP ARRAN NORDKAPP ☼

The loveliest place to stay on the island – just a stone's throw from the Arctic Ocean – with freshly baked bread and pastries for breakfast. *40 rooms | Kamøyvær | tel. 78 47 51 29 | www.arran.as | Moderate*

KIRKEPORTEN CAMPING

This camp site in the northern-most fishing village in the world also has well-insulated cabins and a lake at the door where the charr are just waiting to be hooked. *Skarsvåg | tel. 78 47 52 33 | www.kirkeporten.no | Budget*

Front-row seats for the spectacle of the midnight sun: observation platform at the North Cape

INFORMATION

Turistinformasjon | Fiskeriveien 4 | Honningsvåg | tel. 78 47 70 30 | www. nordkapp.no

Defence complex from the 18th century: Vardøhus Festning

VARANGER

(139 E–F 1–2) (*M–N 1–2***)** ⭐ **There are no trees and no green, only a lot of rocks and boulders on this enormous peninsula in the Arctic Ocean.**

Tana Bru is the hub of East Finnmark. This is where you cross the River Tana that has an exceptional reputation among salmon anglers. The E6 comes from the west and forks off towards Kirkenes. Road 89 lead on to the Barents Sea and *Berlevåg* (135 km/84 mi) and *Båtsfjord* (108 km/ 67 mi). Stay on the 890 – the last 33 km (21 mi), the *Arctic Ocean Road*, between Kongsfjord and Berlevåg are a dream come true: storms, ice and saltwater have eroded the rocks and you will see sandy terraces between them.

Vadsø (pop. 6000; 66 km (42 mi) from Tana Bru) and *Vardø* (pop. 2100; 141 km/ 85 mi) are melting pots of many cultures. In the 18th and 19th centuries, the Kven people came from Finland and sought their luck as farmers, fishermen and mineworkers. Russian factory ships lie at anchor in the harbour at Vardø – symbols of centuries of trade between Norway and Russia.

SIGHTSEEING

HARBOUR BREAKWATERS IN BERLEVÅG

In 1882, a might hurricane wiped out a large portion of the fishing fleet and the Arctic Ocean destroyed valuable property several times at the beginning of the 20th century. The two tetrapod breakwaters built in 1973 are the most important reason that people have remained in Berlevåg. The Hurtigruten ships seek refuge in the harbour when there are extremely strong north winds; if the wind force is normal, you will be able to walk all the way out to the end of the breakwater.

INSIDER TIP ▶ HAMNINGBERG

You reach this virtually deserted fishing village via a fascinating road: 35 km (22 mi) from Vardo with a moonlike landscape on the left-hand side and the Arctic Ocean on the right. You will be able to make out traces of movements in the earth's crust above the many beautiful beaches. A few Hamningbergers still live in the village – which remained unscathed from the destruction of World War II – in summer.

VADSØ MUSEUM

This is where the culture of the Finnish Norwegians (the Kvens) is fostered and passed on. The collections are displayed in a patrician house built in 1850 and a typical Kvene building. *Daily 10am–3pm entrance fee 50 NOK | Hvistendahlgate 31 | www.varangerfmuseum.no*

VARDØHUS FESTNING

This defence complex in Vardø was built between 1734 and 1738 and is now used by the Norwegian Navy. *Daily 8am–9pm | entrance fee 30 NOK | Festningsgaten 20*

FOOD & DRINK

HAVHESTEN RESTAURANT

Reindeer meat? Kamchatka crabs? They taste best directly on the sea: on Ekkerøy, 15 km (9 mi) east of Vadsø. *End of July–mid-Aug | tel. 90 50 60 80 | Moderate*

WHERE TO STAY

BERLEVÅG CAMPING & APPARTEMENT

Simple accommodation with an open view of the sea. Informal atmosphere, good service, places for tents and caravans. *4 rooms, 4 flats | tel. 78 98 16 10 | www.berlevag-pensjonat.no | Budget*

INSIDERTIP FOLDABRUKET ☆

Fish were still landed here in the 1950s and the atmosphere of this time has been preserved. You can catch your fish for breakfast or dinner from your window – however, the seagulls might be a bit loud for you. *8 rooms | Strandveien | Kjøllefjord | tel. 78 49 82 50 | www.foldalbruket.no | Budget*

INFORMATION

Båtsfjord: Frivillighetssentralen | tel. 78 98 34 00 | baatsfjord.frivillig@c2i.net; Berlevåg Pensjonat & Camping AS | tel. 78 98 16 10 | www.berlevag-pensjonat.no; Tana: Turist-informasjon | Rådhusveien 3 | tel. 78 92 53 98 | www.tana.kommune.no; Vadsø: Kirkegata 15 | tel. 78 94 04 44 | www.varanger.com; Vardø: Sentrum | tel. 78 98 69 07 | www.varanger.com

WHERE TO GO

INSIDERTIP SØR-VARANGER/ PASVIKTAL (139 E–F 3–4) (⌂ M–N3)

After a long trip to the east, the E6 ends in *Kirkenes* (pop. 3300). Here, the *Varanger Museum (www.varangermuseum.no)* shows how the region was affected by World War II. The *Pasviktal*, now a national park, lies to the south of the town. A dense primeval forest with a great variety of flora invites you to hike but you should be careful – this is also home to brown bears. 40 km (25 mi) further south, you can look over to the chimneys in Nikel in Russia from *Høyde 96 (Height 96)*. The *Skogfoss Waterfall* is only 50m from the Russian border. In the south of the national park, a heap of stones shows where Russia, Finland and Norway meet (5 km/ 3 mi from the end of the road in *Noatun*). *Information: Turistinformasjon Kirkenes | Sør-Varanger Bibliotek | Torget | tel. 78 97 17 77 | www.kirkenesinfo.no*

LOW BUDGET

▶ The pass for the *Nordkapp Film Festival* (mid-September in Honningsvåg) only costs 425 NOK – a real bargain in expensive Norway. *www.nordkappfilmfestival.no*

▶ The cosy *Mini Pris Motel* (only 15 km/ 9 mi from the North Cape) has double rooms for 375 NOK. Bring your own bedding! *10 rooms | tel. 78 47 52 48 | Skarsvåg | www.minimotellet.no*

▶ In the north, many private people rent out flats in their homes as holiday accommodation. Ask in the local tourist information office!

TRIPS & TOURS

The tours are marked in green in the road atlas, pull-out map and on the back cover

1 THROUGH NORWAY'S FJORDS

Stavanger, the centre of Norway's oil industry, is not a metropolis – but platforms and modern buildings show what is important in the city. The fjords and fjell seem to be far away. But typical West Norway comes into sight with the first ferry: along the fjords of Ryfylke and into the mountains, through tunnels to Hardangerfjord and finally to Sognefjord. This is a journey of a good 450 km (280 mi); allow yourself at least three days.

The ferry for Tau (a 45-min. journey | 25 departures daily) leaves from the centre of Stavanger → p. 62 to take you to the land of the fjords. After you reach the other side, make a detour on Road 13 to the south. Shortly after Jørpeland turn left to Preikestolshytta where the two-hour, somewhat demanding, hike to the famous rocky ☆ Preikestolen → p. 63 plateau begins. The view from the 604m (2000 ft) high 'pulpit' over the Lysefjord and the snow-capped peaks is absolutely dream-like – that is, if the weather is fine.

You have now reached Ryfylke, an area of wide valleys, extensive forests, fjords with many side-arms and mountains stretching

Long routes through breathtaking scenery: you will discover fjords in full bloom and rugged coasts

as far as Setesdal in southern Norway. On your way to the north, make a stopover in **Ardal**. A breathtaking panorama of the valley, the village and fjord opens up from the farm ❀ *Høiland Gard (5 rooms, 4 cabins | tel. 51 75 27 75| post@hoiland-gard.no | Budget–Moderate)*. Only a few kilometres after crossing the **Jøsenfjord** near *Hjelmeland (10-min. ferry crossing | 22 departures daily)* 17 km (11 mi) north

of Årdal, you will have a magnificent view eastwards to the fjord before a short climb takes you to **Erfjord** and **Sandsfjord**.

Before you turn off Road 13 to the east towards the mountain, it is worthwhile making a brief detour to **Sand** (45 km/ 28 mi from Hjelmeland) on the fjord. The regional museum *Ryfylkemuseet* which focuses on everyday life and work in a village on the fjord is housed in a restored boat and net house. The *Brødrene af Sand* sailing ship lies at anchor on the quay. *(Museum and ship mid-June–mid-Aug daily 10am–6pm, at other times Mon–Fri 10am–3.30pm | entrance fee 40 NOK)*. The impressive *Ryfylke Turisthotel (71 rooms | tel. 52 79 27 00 | www.ryfylketuristhotel.no | Expensive)* is located between the marina and mouth of the River Suldalslågel. You can watch salmon and sea trout making their way back upstream in the nearby Salmon Studio.

The difficult stretch of Road 13 along Suldalsvatnet Lake takes you away from the fjords for a while and into the mountains. Near Breifonn (71 km/44 mi from Sand), you meet the E134 to Hardanger. The southern landmark of this traditional holiday area are the Låtefossen falls that plummet down into the river next to the road. The waterfall is 400 m (1300 ft) long

The old hydro-electric power station in Tyssedal

and plunges 165 m (540 ft) straight down into the depths.

Stay on the right when you reach the industrial town of Odda (39 km/24 mi from Breifonn) and stop at the INSIDER TIP *Norwegian Hydroelectric Power and Industry Museum (mid-May–beginning of Sept daily 10am–5pm | entrance fee 70 NOK | www. nvim.no)* in Tysdsedal. The power station is a magnificent, painstakingly restored, building constructed between 1900 and 1920 at a time when water power became the mainstay of Norway's energy production and industrial development.

It is worth making a stop and spending the night in a comfortable cabin *(Hardangertun | tel. 53 67 13 13 | www.hardanger-tun.no | Budget)* in Kinsarvik (41 km/26 mi from Odda). If you are a keen hiker, you can make a climb through the Husedalen Valley past four waterfalls to the Hardangervidda → p. 57 plateau.

After the ferry crossing from Brimnes to Bruravik *(10 min. | 40 departures daily)*, you will not even need an hour before you arrive in Voss (29 km/18 mi from Kinsartvik). This winter sports resort, surrounded by wooded slopes on the shore of a lake, is a popular destination for extreme sports enthusiasts. Don't be surprised if parachutists and paragliders zoom past you on their way down into the valley.

With the Tvindefossen water steps behind you, the climb to the Vikafjellet Pass begins. It is rewarding to make a short or long hike into the mountains from one of the lay-bys on the road.

Shortly before you reach Vik (58 km/36 mi from Voss), turn off and visit Hopperstad stave church *(Hopperstad Stavkirke)* from 1150 with its Gothic altar baldachin decorated with magnificent carvings. On the other side of the road you will see the small Hove stone church (2nd half of the 12th century) – the oldest building on either side of Sognefjord. This is the last stop before reaching **Sognefjord** → p. 59 that you follow for a few minutes until you arrive in **Vangsnes** from where the ferries to *Hella (15 min. | 24 departures daily)* and *Dragsvik (10 min. | 25 departures daily)* depart.

2 NORWAY'S DREAM COAST

Norway's most beautiful circular route starts near Steinkjer north of Trondheim. If you decide to take Road 17 – 'the slow way north' – you should realise that the 578 km (360 mi) and seven ferry crossing will take quite a long time. However, if – after a while – you feel that you don't want to drive any further, this is a clear sign that you are about to lose your heart to this stretch of coast between Trondheim and Bodø. Sandy beaches and waterfalls, the blue sea and fascinating mountains, islands, mighty glaciers and the light of the north – all are waiting for you.

You will see ❄ **Torghatten** Mountain in the distance while you are still at the ❄ ferry terminal in **Vennesund** *(ferry Holm–Vennesund | 20 min. | 15 departures daily)*. Its most striking feature is a hole big enough for 'a whole ship to sail through'. Stay in Vennesund for a while and enjoy the ocean and sunset on Nordland's coast. You can spend the night in *Vennesund Brygge og Camping (3 rorbus, 14 cabins | Sømna | tel. 75 02 73 75 | www.vennesund. no | Budget)*. The next day you will reach **Brønnøysund**, 'the town in the centre of Norway', and Torghatten that can be admired from afar after around 50 km (31 mi). The mountain is actually 15 km (9 mi) away on an island. A 20-minute walk takes you to the 160 m (525 ft) wide and 35 m (115 ft) high hole where you will be greeted with a magnificent view.

Something absolutely unique awaits you 8 km (5 mi) north of Brønnøysund at Tilrem Farm – a herb garden **Hildurs Urterarium** *(June–Aug daily 10am–5pm | entrance fee 30 NOK | www.hildurs.no)*. The Arctic Circle is not far away but here herb soup is served – fresh from the garden. After a 20-minute ferry crossing from Horn to Anndalsvågen *(8 departures daily)* and 17 km (11 mi) on a beautiful coastal road, you will reach **Vevelstad/Forvik**. The 200-year-old INSIDER TIP **Forvikgården** trading place is right at the ferry terminal and a little further on you will see the **local heritage museum** and **church** (1796) with an altar painting by Joseph Pisani.

The next ferry takes one hour to reach Tjøtta and 19 km (12 mi) from there lies **Alstahug**, the heart of Nordland. Further inland the **Seven Sisters** mountain chain can be seen. The red ❄ *Alstahaug parish house (June–mid Aug daily 10am–7pm | entrance fee 70 NOK)* is almost directly on the shore next to the church. Three hundred years ago, this was the home of Petter Dass, Nordland's great poet, whose collection *Nordland's Trumpet* has its place in every Norwegian home library. Thanks to a 1000 m (3300 ft) long suspension bridge, **Sandnessjøen** (pop. 5300), a fishing town on the bank of Alstfjord, can be seen from far away. There you can stay in the *Rica Hotel (69 rooms | Torolv Kveldulvsonsgate 16 | tel. 75 06 50 00 | www.rica. no | Moderate)*.

Here comes the next ferry terminal *(Levang–Nesna | 25 min. | 11 departures daily)*. The mountains loom up closer to the road on the land side. The ferry from Kilboghamn to Jektvik *(1 hour | 5–6 departures daily)* would hardly be anything special if it wasn't for the imaginary Arctic Circle. The captain is sure to tell you when it is reached but you won't notice anything except the perpetual ice that lies in wait as does the next ferry 28 km (18 mi) from Jektvik *(Ågskaret–Forøy | 10 min. | 10 departures daily)*. After such a long drive, there is good reason to stop here for a while: from Holandsfjord, the ❄ Engabreen – an arm of the Svartisen → p. 76 – reaches almost all the way to the sea. An excursion ship from Holand or Braset will bring you close to the furrowed mass of ice. You can spend the night surrounded by the magnificent scenery of Nordland on *Negarden Farm (1 flat | tel. 90 09 67 20 | www.halsa. kommune.no | Moderate)*.

After you pass through Svartisen Tunnel, make your way to the industrial town of Glomfjord and then on to Ørenes. 38 km (24mi) further north, turn on to Road 838 towards ❄ Gildeskål and when you arrive there take a stroll through the village and to the church *(guided tours in the summer season)* that was erected before 1250. The tranquillity, harbour idyll and magical view in all directions are a strong contrast to the raging masses of water of the Saltstraumen → p. 76 that follows and is the perfect climax to our trip through Nordland. Road 17 ends near Løding on Road 80 a few miles beyond the maelstrom that is so spectacular when seen from above and this tour reaches its final destination in Bodø → p. 72. Information on Road 17 can be obtained from *Kystriksveien (Postboks 91 | 7701 Steinkjer | tel. 74 40 17 17 | www.rv17.no)*.

and you will cover a total of 82 km (51 mi) by bike. The trip takes you through rugged mountainous scenery, so be sure to have warm, weatherproof clothing with you! The train leaves the main railway station in Oslo → p. 41 in the morning, passes through the western suburbs of the capital and then the two towns of Drammen and Hønefoss. You will feel that you are climbing upwards for the first time in the dense forests in Hallingdal Valley with its rivers and wooden houses. The slopes in Geilo have been smoothed and you will not find it difficult to imagine how popular this is as a winter sports resort. Your rented bicycles will be waiting to take you on the first section of the Rallar Road → p. 109 at the railway station in Haugastøl, 275 km (172 mi) from Oslo and 988 m (3240 ft) higher up.

After you leave Haugastøl, you cycle for 27 km (17 mi) on a firm, but not tarmaced, road to Finse: the 'roof of Norway' at an altitude of 1222 m (4010 ft) has now been reached! Spend a night in the *Finse Hotel (43 rooms | tel. 56 52 71 00 | www.finse 1222.no | only full board | Expensive)*. This more than 100-year-old mountain hotel has long been popular with mountaineers and hikers – and they have recently been

3 FROM THE CAPITAL CITY TO THE WORLD CULTURAL SITE

● The trip from Oslo to the country of the fjords is possibly even more beautiful if you travel by train or bicycle than by car. You will experience mountain landscapes where there are no roads but good cycle tracks. Start by taking the train from Oslo to Haugastøl and then cycle – in two stages – to Flåm on Aurlandsfjord. You then continue with the famous Flåms scenic railway to Bergen and return to Oslo from there. The tour lasts two days

joined by bike trekkers. Guests exchange tips and make plans for the next day in front of the fireplace or on the ☼ terrace with a view of Hardangerjøkulen glacier.

The second section of the old construction road alongside the Bergen railway actually runs downhill but this does not mean that it is any less strenuous. You can even come across snowdrifts in summer – the weather up here is very changeable and you will see why you need warm clothes. Hardangerjøkulen glacier keeps an eye on the travellers who come here and you will really have to concentrate on some of the bends – especially after Hotel Vathalsen where the adventurous descent into the Flamsdålen valley begins. On the last 10 km (6 mi) of this 55 km (34 mi) stretch, with a difference in altitude of around 800 m, you will be in the lee of massive walls of rock. On both sides, waterfalls tumble into the valley like threads of gossamer and fill the river flowing alongside the hiking path.

You reach Aurlandsfjord, a Unesco World Heritage Site, in Flåm. In summer, you can hear virtually every language spoken in the world in the station of the world famous Flåmsbana → p. 60; the hustle and bustle will be a noticeable contrast to the peace and quiet of the past two days. This is where you return your bicycles. After having lunch on the fjord and visiting the *Flåms Railway Museum (www.flams bana-museet.no)* in the erstwhile station in Flåms, you take the train through 20 tunnels and many narrow bends back into the mountains. After 20 km (12 mi), the electric locomotive has once again reached an altitude of 865 m (2840 ft) – you will be happy that you left your bikes down below at the fjord!

In Myrdal you change to the Bergen railway and head towards Bergen. After a two-hour journey – passing through Voss, countless tunnels and past even more fjords – you finally reach Bergen → p. 52 where your body and soul will be able to recuperate from a day full of wonderful impressions. The trip through southern Norway comes to an end here.

The quickest way to return to Oslo is by train. But, if you have more time, board one of the Hurtigruten ships for Ålesund → p. 48 where you can catch the bus to Åndalsnes and, from there, the train to Oslo.

More information on travel and bookings can be obtained from *Fjord Tours (www. fjordtours.com)* and from the *Norwegian National Railway (www.nsb.no)*.

From Aurlandsfjord to the mountains: the Flåmsbana on its way to Myrdal

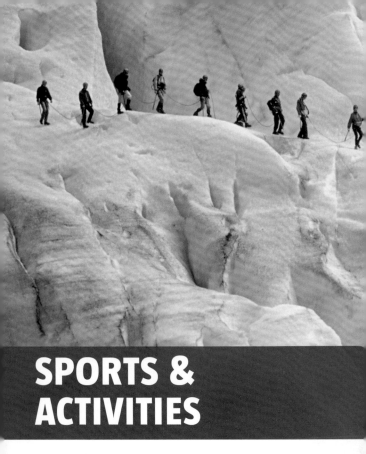

SPORTS & ACTIVITIES

Norway is becoming an increasingly popular destination for people seeking extreme challenges. But Norway also has a lot to offer to those holiday-makers who just want to be on the move.

Coasts and fjords, fantastic rivers and lakes at all altitudes are perfect stomping grounds for anglers and water sports enthusiasts, and the mountains offer challengers to hikers, mountaineers and of course skiers.

ANGLING

Cod, rock salmon, halibut and pollock – and, in summer, mackerel and plaice – can be caught along the coast and out at sea. Pay attention to the export regulations (see 'Travel Tips'). Anglers who want to fish for sea trout and salmon have to obtain a fishing license *(fiskeravgift)* priced at 225 NOK from the post office as well as permission from the leaseholder of the river *(20–100 NOK per day | details from tourist information offices)*. If you want to catch trout or other freshwater fish in a river or lake, you only need permission from the owner. It is only allowed to catch – and keep – two salmon and sea trout within a 24-hour period in the Orkla, Gaula, Stjordalelv and Vedalselv Rivers. *www.visitnorway.com*

Photo: Hiking on Briksdalsbreen, a side-arm of the Jostedalsbreen glacier

Norway's coasts, plateaus and mountains offer a great many possibilities for you to test your fitness

CYCLING

A 450km (280mi)-long bike trail starts at *Andenes* at the northern tip of the Vesterålen and runs to the southern-most point of the Lofoten at Å. You can spend the nights in cabins or *rorbus*; the best times for the tour are May/June and end of August/September. (Description of the route from *Destination Lofoten | tel. 76 06 98 00 | www.* *lofoten.info*). The Jæren region is flat and its sandy beaches endless: ideal for cycling with the family. *Egersund*, where the ferries coming from Denmark dock, is a good starting point. A guide for the North Sea Route can be obtained from all major tourist information offices from Kristiansand to Bergen. The *Rallar Road* includes the towering mountains between Oslo and Bergen. The stretch on the northern edge

Only if you have no fear of heights: mountain biking on Geirangerfjord

of the Hardangervidda will take you through rough mountain terrain and, for this reason, it is not really suitable for young children. You can find descriptions of all the bike trails in Norway and order a practical guide from *www.bike-norway.com*.

EXTREME SPORTS

Running up mountains with or without Nordic walking sticks, jogging in high-tech gear and with heart rate monitors or racing through the uplands on a mountainbike. Where: from tarmaced roads to plateaus. When: at any time of the day or year (with a headlamp in the dark). If you want to be part of this, bring your equipment with

you. In summer there are many open running races – register and join in. The most famous long-distance run is the ● *Birkebeineren (www.birkebeiner.no)* and there are three of them: in March as a 54 km (34 mi) ski race, in August as an almost 100 km (63 mi) off-road bike race, and as a 21 km (13 mi) cross country run in September. The real Birkebeiner cracks take part in all three races between Rena and Lillehammer and get a special diploma for it. The number of participants is restricted and booked out within minutes – so watch the web for the registration date and get on the list right away.

GOLF

There are around 250 golf courses in Norway; sometimes magnificent greens have been created in seemingly inaccessible sites. The most beautiful of all is the nine-hole INSIDER TIP ▶ *Lofoten Golfbane (green fee 300 NOK | tel. 76 07 20 02 | www.lofoten-golf.no)* located directly on the open sea, surrounded by cliffs, on the Lofoten Islands. The season runs from June to October and you will even be able to play under the midnight sun (end of May to mid-July) if the weather cooperates. *Norges Golfforbund | Oslo | tel. 21 02 91 50 | www.golfforbundet.no*

MOUNTAINEERING & HIKING

Space and seclusion can be found all over Norway, from the woods near Oslo to far up north at the Cape. The well-marked trails and simple to comfortable cabins make the high plateaus and islands particularly attractive destinations. Backpackers are especially fond of the *Saltfellet-Svartisen* and *Øvre Pasvik* national parks in Northern Norway, *Bjørgefjell* and *Dovrefjell* in the centre of the country, *Jotun-*

heimen and *Rondane* in the south – and, of course, the *Hardangervidda*. The cabins are usually located three to eight hours walk from each other. You can obtain detailed information from the Norwegian Hiking Association *DNT (Oslo | tel. 22 82 28 22 | www.turistforeningen.no)*.

DNT also provides essential information for mountaineers, climbers & co. The most popular areas are the demanding peaks in the west of *Jotunheimen* and around *Jostedalsbreen* glacier. Glacier hikes with experienced guides are offered there, as well as at *Folgefonna glacier (tel. 95 11 77 92 | www.folgefonnibreforarlag.no)* near Hardangerfjord, throughout the summer. Bergtatt *Stryn (tel. 95 20 11 92 | tel. 95 20 11 92 | www.bergstattstryn.com)* in the western region of Nordfjord is a very good address (for mountainbike tours as well). Local mountaineering clubs can be contacted through the tourist information offices.

SKIING

In a country with so much space there have to be a lot of cross-country trails. They begin in front of the house or cabin door, are often floodlit, and can run for dozens of kilometres. And, you can be sure of there being snow from November to April – at least, east of the fjords and from Nordland to the North Cape. Alpine skiers have also discovered Norway and they can choose from a handful of first-class destinations. *Trysilfjellet (www.skistar. com/trysil)* near the Swedish border is an ideal ski resort for families as is the Olympic town of *Lillehammer. Geilo (www.geilo. no)*, halfway between Oslo and Bergen, offers the best combination of alpine and cross-county skiing. Young alpinists who are into off-slope skiing travel to *Stranda (www.strandafjellet.no)* near Ålesund or *Hemesdal (www.hemesdal.no)*.

WATER SPORTS

The entire south coast from Oslo to Egersund is a superb sailing area and it often gets quite crowded in the harbours. However, you will always be able to find a calm bay where you can drop anchor. The harbours to the north are more sheltered and also have more room.

Canoes and kayaks are even more Norwegian: offers range from tours lasting several days along the coast and in the fjords to trips from lake to lake (with your tent and sturdy shoes in your kit) and white-water courses on one of the rivers that flow from the alpine regions to the east or west. The number one address for this is *Sjoa*, a tributary of the Lågen in the upper Gudbrandsdalen region. There are half, one or two-day tours. *(Information: Sjoa Rafting | Heidal | tel. 90 07 10 11 | www. sjoarafting.com)*.

You will get a taste of the Arctic if you take part in one of the kayak tours on the `INSIDER TIP` *glacial lakes at Jostedalsbreen (Breheimsenteret Jostedal | tel. 97 01 43 70 | www.icetrol.com)*.

Kayak tour in the skerries

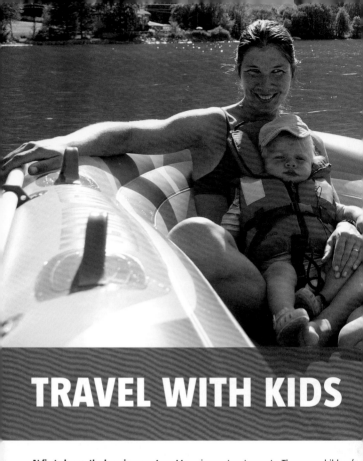

TRAVEL WITH KIDS

At first glance, the long journey to get to Norway, the enormous distances in the country itself and the high prices might make you think that Norway is not really the place for a family holiday. Nevertheless, many parents set off for the north with their children on the back seat year after year.

It is also not so difficult if you decide to use public transport: many trains have family compartments and open-plan carriages with play corners. These can also be found on all of the ferries to Norway, the major ferries on the fjords and Hurtigruten ships. Baby-care rooms and highchairs are taken for granted – even

in most restaurants. There are children's menus and nobody minds children playing. Norway is a country that loves children. Most families prefer to spend their holidays in a cabin. There are enough bedrooms, rustic furnishing and small playgrounds near the house are standard. The television will be almost completely ignored: children want to enjoy themselves outdoors and there is plenty of that in Norway.

Zoos and theme parks, aquariums, riding schools, farms, safe beaches in the interior and on the coast – or boundless sledging and skiing in the Norwegian winter – ensure that there will never be even a hint of boredom.

Holidays in summer or winter are a lot of fun: there is always something new waiting to be discovered in this country with so much space

A trip to Norway does require a certain amount of planning. The enormous distances, the lack of urban attractions and the possibility of rainy weather can make the young ones a bit restless. Tip: park the car and travel part of the way with one of the Hurtigruten ships or take a catamaran to a fishing village on one of the islands. The hustle and bustle on the quay usually keeps children interested.

THE SOUTH

INSIDER TIP EVENTYRFABRIKKEN
(133 E5) (*D17*)

The largest covered playground in Norway is located close to the E6. It is a five-storey jungle of bouncy castles, trampolines, ladders, tunnels and many other games. There is also a café. *Mon–Thu noon–8pm, Fri 11am–8pm, Sat/Sun 10am–8pm | en-*

KRISTIANSAND DYREPARK
(132 C6) (*M B18*)

Located 11 km (7 mi) east of Kristiansand, this is the only real zoo in Norway and is home to around 800 animals and birds. You should also visit the people living in Kardemomme: the children's book *When the Robbers came to Cardamom Town* by Thorbjørn Egner has become reality in this miniature town. *Beginning of July–beginning of Aug daily 10am–7pm | entrance fees, adults 370 NOK, children (3–14 years) 290 NOK | www.dyreparken.no*

INSIDER TIP NATURHISTORISK MUSEUM (133 E4) (*M D16*)

The skeletons of prehistoric animals are really fascinating! The 47-million-year-old primate 'Ida' has made the Oslo museum a real hit with the public. The Botanical Garden with its scented garden is the perfect place to take the children for a picnic on a warm summer day. *Museum Tue–Sun 11am–4pm | garden mid-March–Sept Mon–Fri 7am–9pm, Sat/Sun 10am–9pm, at other times to 5pm | entrance fees, adults 50 NOK, children (4–16) 25 NOK, families 100 NOK | Sarsgate 1 | www.nhm.uio.no*

BØ SØMMARLAND
(133 D4) (*M C17*)

Northern Europe's largest water fun park is located in the beautiful high hills of the Telemark region. Especially in summer, this is an ideal place to spend an entire day. The children can really let their hair down on the enormous water-mountain-and-valley run, as well as a gigantic half-pipe and artificial surfing wave. Of course, you can just go for a swim here or relax in the sun – but it is hardly worth paying the rather high entrance fee just for that. *End of June–mid-Aug daily 10am–7pm | entrance fees, adults 350 NOK, children (3–4½ ft tall) 295 NOK, under 95cm, free | Steintjønnvegen 2 | Bø | www.sommarland.no*

A good team: young researchers in their element

trance fees, adults free, children up to 16 125 NOK (3 hours) | Vestengveien 40 | Sarpsborg | www.eventyrfabrikken.no*

INSIDER TIP HUNDEFOSSEN FAMILY PARK (133 D–E2) (*M D15*)

This is where the world's biggest troll lives – he is 14 metres (46 ft) high (when sitting down) – there is also a fairy-tale castle and grotto, a wax museum, car tracks and a place for swimming. The energy centre provides informative entertainment and shows how electricity is produced using water power. *Mid-June–end of Aug daily 10am–7pm, at other times 10am–3pm | entrance fees, adults 340 NOK, children (90–120cm) 275 NOK | in Fåberg, 13km (8mi) north of Lillehammer on the E6 | www.hunderfossen.no*

THE WEST

ATLANTIC PARK IN ÅLESUND
(134 A5) (🕮 B13)

Several landscaped aquariums have been carefully imbedded in the maritime environment of Norway's most modern aquarium. The largest pool contains 4 million litres of water and is the home of all of the species of fish that live off the coast of Western Norway. The daily highlight is when a diver goes underwater to feed the fish. *June–Aug Sun–Fri 10am–7pm, Sat 10am–4pm, at other times, daily 11am–4pm | entrance fee, adults 130 NOK, children 65 NOK | Teeniest | Ålesund | www.atlanterhavsparken.no*

VILVITE THEME CENTRE
(132 A3) (🕮 A15)

This interactive science centre is located in Bergen on the E39 in the hills to the south of the city. Here, children and youths will be able to immerse themselves in the world of natural science and technology. Among the many subjects dealt with are the weather, energy and the ocean. With experiments, an underwater world, ship and oil rig simulators, café and shop. *End of June–mid-Aug daily 10am–5pm, at other times Tue–Fri 9am–3pm, Sat/Sun 10am–5pm | entrance fee, adults 135 NOK, children (3–15 years) 90 NOK | Thormøhlens gate 51 | www.vilvite.no*

LOFOTEN

LOFOTAKVARIET (136 B3) (🕮 F7)

Mainly animals that live in the North Sea swim in the pools of the Lofoten Aquarium near Svolvær. Children are particularly fond of the sea otters and seals. *June–Aug daily 10am–6pm, at other times, Sun–Fri 11am–3pm | entrance fee, adults 110 NOK, children 55 NOK, families 310 NOK | Kabelvåg | Storvågen district | www.lofotakvariet.no*

TROMS

POLARIA (138 A3) (🕮 G5)

A fantastic information and adventure centre in Tromsø: in addition to the wide-screen cinema with a film about the polar regions, there is an aquarium and a seal pool, as well as exhibitions on polar research. *In summer daily 10am–7pm, at other times, noon–5pm | entrance fee, adults 100 NOK, children 50 NOK, families 250 NOK | Hjalmar Johansensgate 12 | www.polaria.no*

POLAR ZOO TROMS (137 D2) (🕮 G6)

This zoo lies around 70 km (44 mi) north of Narvik in the Salangsdalen valley. The 'polar' animal life includes the elk, musk oxen and reindeer as well as wolves, lynxes, foxes, wolverines, brown bears and badgers. *June–Aug daily 9am–6pm | entrance fee, adults 215 NOK, children (3–15 years) 125 NOK, families 600 NOK | Bardu (E6, signposted from Fossbakken) | www.polarzoo.no*

The biggest troll in the world in Hunderfossen Family Park

FESTIVALS & EVENTS

PUBLIC HOLIDAYS

1 January, *New Year's Day*; **1 May**, *Labour Day*; **Maundy Thursday**; **Good Friday**; **Easter Monday**; **17 May**, *Constitution Day (National Holiday)*; **Ascension**, **Whit Monday**; **25 & 26 December**, *Christmas* (celebrations take place from the afternoon of 24 December until Boxing Day)

FESTIVALS & EVENTS

JANUARY

▶ *International Film Festival Tromsø:* The festival season starts in icy cold and complete darkness. You can see the northern lights and an excellent programme of films that were not produced in Hollywood. Second week in January. *www.tiff.no*

MARCH/APRIL

▶ *Holmenkollen Ski Festival in Oslo:* As many as 50,000 spectators make the competition from the famous Holmenkollen jump a real carnival. Second weekend in March. *www.holmenkollen-worldcup.no*
▶ **INSIDER TIP** *Vossajazz:* Anybody interested in experiencing the perfect synthe-sis between international folk music and jazz should visit Voss on the weekend before Easter. *www.vossajazz.no*
▶ ★ *Easter Festival in Kautokeino and Karasjok:* The Sami festival with family festivities, concerts, theatre performances, snow-scooter and reindeer races. *www.samieasterfestival.org*

MAY/JUNE

May 17 is ▶ ★ ● *Constitution Day* (National Holiday) in Norway. The festivities in Oslo – including a procession of children to the palace – and Bergen are especially impressive. The decorations always include fresh birch twigs along with the national flag.
▶ *Bergen Festival (www.fib.no)* and
▶ *Nattjazz* (Night Jazz): Bergen really lets its hair down for ten days from the end of May to the beginning of June. Top artists from all over the world, free concerts, and music in the streets.

JUNE

The ▶ *Hardanger Music Festival* with folk music, chamber and church music, is held on the first weekend in June in a landscape in which Edvard Grieg composed many of

Music and more: there is a lot to celebrate between winter and the summer solstice – and jazz fans really get their money's worth

his best-known works. *www.hardanger musikfest.no*

▶ *Midsummer Night* is celebrated throughout Norway on 23 June with bonfires and a great deal of alcohol.

At the end of June, the ▶ INSIDER TIP *Risør Chamber Music Festival* takes place. During these five days concerts are given by both up-and-coming performers and international stars. All of this in the setting of swaying boats, the blue of the Skagerrak and the white houses of the small town; shrimps and white wine are served on the quay. *www.kammermusikkfest.no*

JULY

▶ *Moldejazz* is still the biggest and – in terms of the surroundings – most beautiful of all the Norwegian jazz festivals. This is where world-famous artists and club bands appear and there are concerts on street corners, in small bars and even on a stage in the open-air museum. In the third week in July in Molde. *www.moldejazz.no*

▶ *Battle of Stiklestad*: Events that took place in 1030 when Olav lost his life fighting for the crown are revived in the 'Saint Olav's Play' performed in an open air museum near Verdal north of Trondheim. In the last week in July. *www.stiklestad.no*

AUGUST

In the second week in August, treats for the ears and palate come together during the ▶ *Sildajazz Festival* held in the small town of Haugesund in Western Norway. There is jazz on the streets and in the pubs, and a great variety of herrings at the harbour. *www.sildajazz.no*

The ▶ *Øyafestival* in the Mediaeval Park (Middelalderparken) in Oslo has developed into the best open-air rock festival in Norway. On the second weekend in August. *www.oyafestival.com*

LINKS, BLOGS, APPS & MORE

LINKS

▶ www.visitnorway.com Official website of the Norwegian Tourist Board (Innovation Norway). Comprehensive information about nature, destinations, cities, accommodation, holidays, camping and all the places you plan to visit – and others you will have on your list for your next trip.

▶ www.norway.org.uk Norway's official website in the UK which has information on planning a trip to Norway, embassy and consulate details, studying or working there as well as facts and figures about the country, its culture and history (www.norway.org for the USA site).

▶ www.tnp.no This is the website of Norway's English language newspaper in *The Norway Post*. It caters to the international community and has local and international news as well as sections for art, culture, health and a multimedia section with videos and photographs. You can also follow their updates via Facebook and Twitter.

VIDEOS & PODCASTS

▶ www.visitnorway.com/your way A link from the official travel guide site connects you to a wide selection of excellent videos featuring hikes, cruises, kayak trips, nature and history.

▶ http://itunes.apple.com/us/podcast/one-minute-norwegian These *One Minute Norwegian* podcasts by Radio Lingua Network are quick one minute lessons to help tourists in Norway to get by with just enough Norwegian words and phrases to charm the locals.

▶ Vimdeo.com/2269307 Here you will find poetic images of all of the moods of the ever-changing heavens above Norway. One of the many comments on the site even goes so far as to say that: 'If nature was a script, the director shooting the film would have to be a poet.' When thinking about Norway, one can only agree wholeheartedly with these feelings.

Whether you are still getting ready for your trip or are already in Norway, you will find more valuable information, videos and networks to add to your holiday experience at these links

VIDEOS & PODCASTS

▶ www.youtube.com/watch?v=Vd09-1HaOxg Although this clip of an extensive tour through the regions of South and Middle Norway dates from the year 2009, it is guaranteed to bring back memories for those who have visited the area themselves and make those who have not think about where to spend their next holidays.

APPS

▶ Navmii GPS Norway HD Navigation software for your iPad to make sure that you don't lose your way on any of the roads between the Skagerrak and Arctic Circle.

▶ Oslo (Norway) Map Offline This provides an extremely useful map of the city of Oslo that can even be used offline. It is in English and can be accessed from your iPhone or iPad.

BLOGS & FORUMS

▶ www.newsinenglish.no View and News from Norway is a blog and news site set up by the Californian ex-editor of the Norwegian *Aftenposten* after it stopped its English language service. The site reports on issues of interest to the expat community and it also has a rather quirky link to Moose News which features moose-related articles.

▶ www.ninside.org Norway International Network is a 'dynamic and inclusive association with the goal of building a social and professional network'. Networking opportunities are provided through their meetings, online forums and discussion groups. The network also organises social activities.

NETWORK

▶ www.couchsurfing.org/mapsurf.html This extremely innovative site will be especially beneficial for all those adventurous tourists who don't book in advance. Here, you will find a list of people in most of the major towns and villages who have a free bed or sofa and are more than happy to put up guests for the night.

▶ www.travbuddy.com/Norway-travel-guide-c215 This is a perfect internet address for anybody who is looking for somebody to travel with and also helps find friendly Norwegians who want to make interested people from abroad aware of all their country has to offer. You will find guides and tips to more than 650 individual destinations including many out-of-the-way places most tourists do not visit.

TRAVEL TIPS

ARRIVAL

A number of different airlines offer regular flights from the UK to Norway, some of which are surprisingly cheap. British Ariways *(www.britishairways.com)* and SAS *(www.flysas.com)*, as well as the no-frills airlines Norwegian Air Shuttle *(www.norwegian.com)* and Ryanair *(www.ryanair.com/de)*, among others, fly out of various British airports to Oslo, Bergen, Haugesund, Stavanger and Trondheim. It is worth noting that 'Oslo' Torp is around 80 miles from central Oslo; the main Gardemoen International airport is much closer and benefits from a fast train service.

RESPONSIBLE TRAVEL

It doesn't take a lot to be environmentally friendly whilst travelling. Don't just think about your carbon footprint whilst flying to and from your holiday destination but also about how you can protect nature and culture abroad. As a tourist it is especially important to respect nature, look out for local products, cycle instead of driving, save water and much more. If you would like to find out more about eco-tourism please visit: *www.ecotourism.org*

There are also a number flights to Norway from Scotland, in particular from Aberdeen, which service the oil industry.

Flights to and from the US and Canada go via Copenhagen, Stockholm or other European airports.

The last car ferry route between the UK and Norway (Newcastle to Bergen) was withdrawn in September 2008. However several ferries operate between Norway and mainland Europe (e.g. to Denmark; *www.norwaydirect.com*). Most operators offer package deals for a car and passengers, and most lines offer concessions. An additional charge is normally made for bicycles and boats.

Travelling from London to Norway by train is possible but takes a long time. If you take a lunchtime Eurostar to Brussels, a connecting high-speed train to Cologne, the overnight train to Copenhagen and connecting trains to Oslo, you arrive in the evening the day after leaving London.

An InterRail Pass can be recommended for a trip to Scandinavia *(www.interrailnet.com)*. The InterRail Norway Pass is available for 3, 4, 6 or 8 'flexi' days within one month and costs from £109 (35% discount for those under 26). With the pass you can use some bus and ferry lines free of charge and there are reductions on many ship and bus routes.

BANKS & MONEY

Banks are open from 9am to 3.30pm on weekdays, Thu until 5pm (25 NOK fee for currency exchange). The fees are higher in hotels – and the exchange rate much worse.

There are many cash dispensers. Master Card and Visa are accepted in most hotels, restaurants, garages and major shops. There are no limits to the amount of foreign cash that can be brought into the country.

From arrival to time zones

Holiday from start to finish: the most important addresses and information for your Norway trip

CUSTOMS

Your luggage will be checked through to your final destination but the traveller must collect it at the first Norwegian airport, take it through customs and hand it in again at a domestic flight counter. It is worth buying things at the duty-free shop: more than half of the 25 percent VAT will be refunded at the border. There are around 3000 tax-free shops in Norway. The minimum purchase is 310 NOK and the goods must be in their original packing. Remember to ask for a *Global Refund Cheque* when making your purchases. Hunting weapons must be declared.

People of 18 years of age can import alcohol but you have to be at least 20 to bring in spirits; the limits are 1 L of spirits, 1.5 L of wine and 2 L of beer. It is forbidden to export plants and rare animals (including the eggs of threatened bird species). Exports of fish and fish products are limited to 15 kg.

The following articles can be imported tax-free into the EU: 200 cigarettes or 50 cigars or 250 grams of tobacco, 1 L of spirits with more than 22 percent alcoholic content or 2 litres with less, as well as goods valued at £ 145.

DOMESTIC FLIGHTS

The Dash 8s of the Widerøe Airline land in the most remote corners of the country. SAS flies to the major airports. If you plan to travel in summer, it is a good idea to check the internet *(www.sas.no | www. norwegian.no | www.wideroe.no)* or make inquiries in a travel agency.

BUDGETING

Hot dog	from 18 NOK	
	at most petrol stations and snack bars	
Coffee	from 19 NOK	
	for a cup	
Beer	from 62 NOK	
	for ½ L in a restaurant	
Salmon	138 NOK	
	for 1kg of smoked salmon	
Petrol	approx. 10.70 NOK	
	for 1 litre of regular petrol	
Pullover	from 1400 NOK	
	for a genuine Norwegian pullover	

DRIVING IN NORWAY

The maximum speed in built-up areas is 50 km/h (in residential areas, often 30), on motorways 90, on main roads 80, with a caravan 70 km/h (without brakes 60). Dipped headlights are obligatory at all times. It is compulsory for everybody to wear seatbelts and children under the age of four require special seats. Passing points on single-lane roads are indicated with an 'M'. In winter, good winter tyres and snow chains are essential. Toll roads: The *bompenger* ranges from 10 to 160 NOK (for bridges and tunnels). Most toll stations have an automatic fee collection system and some have lanes for AutoPASS and manual payment. *Information on closed roads: tel. 175* (the computer only speaks Norwegian at the beginning but don't hang up!). *NAF Automobile Club breakdown assistance: tel. 81 00 05 05*

ELECTRICITY

220 volt alternating current with the (type C & F) Europlug.

EMBASSIES & CONSULATES

BRITISH EMBASSY
Thomas Heftyesgate 8 | 0264 Oslo | tel.: (47) 23 13 27 00 | www.ukinnorway.fco.gov. uk/en/

EMBASSY OF THE UNITED STATES
Henrik Ibsens gate 48 | 0244 Oslo | switchboard: (47) 21 30 85 40 | norway. usembassy.gov

EMBASSY OF CANADA
Wergelandsveien 7 (4th floor) | 0244 Oslo | (47) 22 99 53 00 | www.canada international.gc.ca/norway

EMERGENCY SERVICES

Police: tel. 112 | Fire brigade: tel. 110 Medical emergencies: tel. 113

EVERYMAN'S RIGHT

The *Allemannsrett* permits everybody to move freely in the non-cultivated country-side – even on private property – and spend up to two nights there. People, animals and nature must not be disturbed in any way and you must keep a distance of at least 150 m to the next inhabited house. Certain sections of the law have been rescinded in some national parks.

HEALTH

Almost all medication requires a prescription. A foreign prescription won't do you any good in Norway so take any important medication you need with you. Headache tablets and nose drops, however, can be bought at the cash deck in food shops. All major towns have a community *legevakt* (medical station). If you have a European Health Insurance Card (EHIC) you will have to pay the same excess as Norwegians (132 NOK; 225 NOK in the evening or at night). Dentists must be paid in full (350–1500 NOK). There are ticks in Norway. For information on vaccinations for travellers, medical treatment and emergency contacts, see *http://goscandinavia.about. com/od/norwa1/tp/norwayhealth.htm).* In the interior and in Finnmark, mosquito nets and a good mosquito cream are essential.

HOTELS & CABINS

Hotel rooms are usually cheaper in summer and hotel passes such as the Nordic Hotel Pass give you additional discounts. But, even if you don't have a pass, ask for lower rates. In the larger cities a double room costs 900–1200 NOK per night, without discount, and an average of 750 NOK in smaller hotels and pensions. Small hotels in the countryside frequently have lower prices. All hotels provide sumptuous breakfast buffets.

Gjestgiveri, pensjon and *fjellstue* offer budget overnight stays outside cities. The latter are the hikers' favourites – along with the cabins run by the *DNT (Den Norske Turistforeningen | www.turistfore-ningen.no | discounts with DNT card for 510 NOK)* – and hotel comforts are starting to make themselves felt even here. There are all standards of cabins: the most basic for 4–5 people costs from 2500 NOK per week in the off-season (up to 8000 NOK in the high season). The simplest camping cabin costs 280 NOK per night, larger ones with bath and kitchen as much as 900 NOK.

Rorbus are traditional Norwegian coastal dwellings. These fishing huts stand right on the water and some of them are even built on stilts. There are a great many on the Lofoten – and, if you make it that far, you should spend some time in one of the most popular fishing villages in the group of islands: in *Henningsvær (tel. 76 06 60 00 | www.henningsvaer-rorbuer. no)*. A beautiful *rorbu* complex can also be found on the island of *Sotra* off the coast of Bergen *(Glesvær Rorbu | tel. 91 56 19 48 | www.glesver-rorbu.no)*.

INFORMATION

www.visitnorway.com provides useful information to help you plan your Norwegian adventure. *Charles House | 5 Lower Regent Street | London SW1Y 4LR | tel: +44 (0) 20 7389 8800*

www.norway.org is Norway's official internet portal providing information on travelling, culture, politics and social matters, as well as studying and working in Norway.

There are good sites on West Norway and the fjords *(www.fjordnorway.com)* and the three most northern administrative regions *(www.visitnorthnorway.com)*. *www.olavsrosa.no* gives information on the major sights and *www.senorge.no* the current weather.

MEDIA

Many cabins have television and satellite antennas. In the *Narvesen* kiosks in Oslo, Bergen and other major cities, you will find a selection of English-language newspapers and magazines.

PUBLIC TRANSPORT

BUSES

Norway has many cross-country, regional and local buses that reach every corner of the country *(connections: www.nor-way.no)*.

FERRIES

Schedules for the regional ferry companies: for *West Norway www.tide.no | www.fjord1.no; for Central Norway www.rva7.no; for North Norway www.veolia-transport.no*.

TRAINS

The network of the Norwegian National Railway (NSB) with almost 4300 km (3400 mi) is not very tightly knit but, especially when travelling long distances, a train journey can be a lot of fun (generous open-plan carriages, comfortable seats and beds). It is a good idea to plan well ahead: tickets available for 199 NOK if purchased 90 days in advance, if you wait longer this rises to 299 and later to 399 NOK.

ORGANIC FOOD

There are around 3000 registered producers of organic products – mainly food – in Norway with almost 6000 products recognised by the Debio organic branch organisation. It is not always easy to find these goods, which are marked with and Ø or *Økologisk*, in low-price supermarkets. Organic food is mainly produced from the Norwegian staples milk, eggs and flour and, on average, is 10–15 percent more expensive than normal products. Supported by the government, an increasing number of agricultural enterprises are attempting to market their goods stressing that they have only travelled a short distance and are therefore environmentally friendly.

PHONES & MOBILE PHONES

Norway has always been a step ahead in the field of telecommunications. Today, there are only about 400 red telephone boxes left; you pay with 1, 5 and 10 crown coins. All telephone numbers have eight digits, there are no dialling codes. The code for calling Norway from abroad is 0047. To call other countries from Norway, dial the country code (UK 0044, US 001, Ireland 00353), the dialling code without 0 and then the telephone number. With your mobile phone, only the country code without 00 is required.

CURRENCY CONVERTER

£	NOK	NOK	£
10	89	100	11.25
20	178	200	22.50
30	267	300	33.75
40	356	400	45
50	445	500	56.25
60	534	600	67.50
70	623	700	78.75
80	712	800	90
90	801	900	101.25

$	NOK	NOK	$
10	59	100	17
20	118	200	34
30	177	300	51
40	236	400	68
50	295	500	85
60	354	600	102
70	413	700	119
80	472	800	136
90	531	900	153

For current exchange rates see www.xe.com

In Norway, there are more mobile phone subscriptions than Norwegians but renting a phone is complicated and cannot be recommended. The price for 'normal' phone calls is sinking. You can find comparatively economical prepaid cards under *mycards.pushline.com*. The most-used prepaid card in Norway is available from Lebara *(www.lebara-mobile.de)*.

PRICES & CURRENCY

100 Norwegian Kroner (NOK) are the equivalent of around £ 11.25 or US$17. It is subdivided into 100 øre. Purchasing power is not one of Norway's strong points and this is particularly apparent when buying food.Having fun is expensive business, too: half a litre of beer in a pub costs at least 65 NOK, a good meal 240 NOK with an additional 315 NOK for a bottle of wine.

SMOKING

It is not permitted to smoke in public buildings and other places open to the public.

TIME

Norway is one hour ahead of Greenwich Mean Time, six hours ahead of US Eastern Time and eight hours behind Australian Eastern Time.

TIPPING

You should only tip if the service warrants it (maximum: 10 percent).

VINMONOPOLET

The age limit for purchasing beer and wine is 18 years and for spirits 20. Alcoholic drinks with an alcohol content of more than 4.75 % (strong ale, wine and spirits) are only sold at state owned alcohol shops, the *Vinmonopolet* (The Wine Monopoly). They typically close earlier than other shops, normally on weekdays at 6pm and on Sat at 3pm. Drinking in public is prohibited. To enjoy a glass or two you must be on private property.

WEATHER, WHEN TO GO

The climate is the same as the Norwegian countryside: it changes all the time and is rather unpredictable. You can trust the forecasts for up to three days ahead but even then you must make sure that they apply to your holiday region. In a country that stretches for 1800 km (1125 mi) and has a mighty mountain range as a weather divide, it comes as no surprise that the east and west, the north and south, very rarely have the same weather.

An Atlantic low in the south, a Siberian high in the north – not at all unusual and at least an invitation to move a few hundred kilometres north for a while. The climatic instability will also affect your luggage: be prepared for rain and soggy ground when you are hiking in the middle of summer. And, even if the weather is calm, make sure that lifejackets, maps and GPS are always at hand when you are on a boat tour.

YOUTH HOSTELS

There are around 70 youth hostels *(vandrerhjem)* in Norway. Beds cost 150 NOK for members; non-members pay an additional 25 NOK. Breakfast or a lunch packet is available for 50 NOK. More information is available on the internet under *www.vandrerhjem.no | or Norske Vandrerhjem (Haralds-heimveien 4 | Box 53 | Grefsen | 0409 Oslo | tel. 23 12 45 10*

WEATHER IN OSLO

	Jan	Feb	March	April	May	June	July	Aug	Sept	Oct	Nov	Dec
Daytime temperatures in °C/°F	−2/28	−1/30	4/39	10/50	16/61	20/68	22/72	21/70	16/61	9/48	3/37	0/32
Nighttime temperatures in °C/°F	−7/19	−7/19	−4/25	1/34	6/43	10/50	13/55	12/54	8/46	3/37	−1/30	−4/25
Sunshine hours/day	2	3	4	6	7	8	7	7	5	3	1	1
Precipitation days/month	8	7	5	7	7	10	11	11	10	10	12	10
Water temperature in °C/°F	3	2	3	5	9	13	16	17	15	11	7	5

USEFUL PHRASES NORWEGIAN

PRONUNCIATION

In this guide to phrases in the main Norwegian language, *bokmål*, simplified assistance in pronouncing the words has been added in square brackets. Note also that the vowel marked 'ü' in the pronunciation guide is spoken as 'ee' with rounded lips, like the 'u' in French 'tu', -e at the end of a word is a syllable spoken like the 'e' in 'the', and 'g' is pronounced as in 'get'.

IN BRIEF

Yes/No/Maybe	Ja/Nei/Kanskje [ya/nayi/kansh-e]
Please	Vær så snill [vair sho snill]
Thank you	Takk [tak]
Excuse me, please/ Pardon?	Unnskyld [ünnshüll]/Hva sa du? [va sa dü]
May I ...?/	Kan jeg ...? [kann yayi]
I would like to .../	Jeg vil gjerne ... [yayi vill yern-e]/
Have you got ...?	Har du (noen) ... ? [har dü (nuen)]
How much is ...	Hva koster ... ? [va koster]
I (don't) like that	Det liker jeg (ikke) [de leeker yayi [ick-e)]
good/bad/broken/	bra [bra]/dårlig [dorli]/ødelagt [erdelagt]/
doesn't work	fungerer ikke [fungerer ick-e]
too much/much/little	for mye [for mü-e]/mye [mü-e]/lite [leet-e]
all/nothing	alt [alt]/ingenting [ingenting]
Help!/Attention!/	Hjelp! [yelp]/Pass på! [pass po]/
Caution!	Forsiktig! [forzikti]
ambulance/police/fire brigade	sykebil [zük-e-beel]/politi [politi]/
	brannvesen [brannvayzen]
prohibition/forbidden	Forbud/forbudt [forbütt]
danger/dangerous	Fare [far-e]/farlig [farli]

GREETINGS, FAREWELL

Good morning!/afternoon/	God morgen! [gu morn]/God dag! [gu dag]/
Hello!	Hei! [high]
Good evening!/night!	God kveld! [gu kvell]/God natt! [gu natt]
goodbye!/See you	Ha det! [ha de]
My name is ...	Jeg heter ... [yayi hayter]
What's your name?	Hva heter du? [va hayter dü]
I'm from ...	Jeg er fra ... [yayi er fra]

Snakker du norsk?

"Do you speak Norwegian?" This guide will help you to say the basic words and phrases in Norwegian.

DATE AND TIME

Monday/Tuesday	mandag [mandag]/tirsdag [teersdag]
Wednesday/Thursday	onsdag [unsdag]/torsdag [toorsdag]
Friday/Saturday	fredag[fraydag]/lørdag [lerdag]
Sunday/working day	søndag [zerndag]/ukedag[ük-edag]
holiday	helligdag [hellidag]
today/tomorrow/yesterday	i dag [ee dag]/i morgen [ee morn]/i går [ee gor]
hour/minute	time [teem-e]/minutt [minütt]
day/night/week	dag [dag]/natt[natt]/uke [ük-e]
month/year	måned [mon-ed]/år [oar]
What time is it?	Hva er klokken? [va air klocken?]
It's three o'clock/	Klokken er tre [klocken air tre]/
It's half past three	Klokken er halv fire [klocken air hal feer-e]

TRAVEL

open/closed	åpent [opent]/stengt [stengt]
entrance/vehicle entrance	inngang [ingang]/innkjørsel [inkyersel]
exit/vehicle exit	utgang [ütgang]/utkjørsel [ütkyersel]
departure/arrival	avgang [avgang]/ankomst [ankommst]
toilets	toaletter [twaletter]
Where is ...?/Where are ...?	Hvor er ...? [voor air]
left/right	venstre [venstr-e]/høyre [her-ir-e]
straight ahead/back	rett fram [rett fram]/tilbake [tillbaak-e]
close/far	nært [nairt]/langt (unna) [langt (ünna)]
bus/tram	buss [büss]/trikk [trick]
underground/taxi/cab	T-bane [te-baan-e]/drosje [drosh-e]
stop/cab stand	stoppested [stopp-e-sted]/ drosjeholdeplass [drosh-e-holleplass]
parking lot/ parking garage	parkeringsplass [parkeringsplass]/ parkeringshus[parkeringshüss]
street map/map	bykart [bükart]/kart [kart]
train station/ harbour/airport	jernbanestasjon [yernbaan-e-stashon]/ havn [haavn]/flyplass [flüplass]
ticket/supplement	billett [beelett]/påslag [poshlag]
single/return	enkel [enkel]/tur-retur [tür-retür]
train/track/platform	tog [tog]/spor [spoor]/rute [rüt-e]
I would like to rent ...	Jeg vil gjerne leie ... [yayi vill yern-e ly-e]
a car/a bicycle/a boat	en bil [en beel]/sykkel [zükkel]/båt [boat]
petrol/gas station	bensinstasjon [benzinstashon]
breakdown/repair shop	skade/verksted [shaad-e/vairksted]

FOOD & DRINK

Could you please book a table for tonight for four?	Vi vil gjerne bestille et bord for fire personer til i kveld. [vee vill yairn-e bestill-e et boor for feer-e perzooner till ee kvell]
The menu, please	Kan jeg få menyen? [kann yayi fo menü-en]
Could I please have ...?	Kunne jeg få ... ? [künn-e yayi fo]
salt/pepper/sugar	salt [zalt]/pepper [pepper]/sukker [zucker]
vinegar/oil	eddik [eddick]/olje [uly-e]
milk/cream/lemon	melk [melk]/fløte [flert-e]/sitron [zitroon]
with/without ice	med [may]/uten is [üten eess]
vegetarian/allergy	vegetarianer [vegetarianer]/allergi [allergee]
May I have the bill, please?	Jeg vil gjerne betale [yayi vill yairn-e betal-e]

SHOPPING

I'd like .../	Jeg vil gjerne ... [yayi vill yairn-e]/
I'm looking for ...	Jeg leter etter ... [yayi layter etter]
pharmacy/chemist	apotek/parfymeri [apotayk/parfümeree]
baker/market	bakeri [backeree]/torget [torg]
shopping centre/	handlesenter [hand-le-zenter]/
department store	varehus [var-e-hüs]
supermarket	supermarked [süpermark-ed]
more/less	mer [mair]/mindre [mindr-e]
organically grown	biologisk dyrket [bioologish dürket]

ACCOMMODATION

I have booked a room	Jeg har bestilt et rom [yai har bestilt ett room]
single room	enkeltrom [enkeltroom]
double room	dobbeltrom [dobbeltroom]
breakfast/half board/	frokost [frookost]/halvpensjon [halpanshon]/
full board (American plan)	fullpensjon [füllpanshon]
the front/	mot framsiden [moot frammzeeden]/
seafront/	mot sjøen [moot shern]/
lakefront	mot innsjøen [moot innshern]
key/room card	nøkkel/nøkkelkort [nerckel/nerckelkoort]
luggage/suitcase/	bagasje [bagash-e]/koffert [kooffert]/
bag	veske [vesk-e]/bag [beg]

BANKS, MONEY & CREDIT CARDS

bank/ATM	bank [bank]/minibank [minibank]
pin code	bankkode [bankkood-e]
I'd like to change ...	Jeg vil gjerne veksle ... [yayi vill yairn-e vek-sle ...]

cash/credit card	kontant [kontant]/kredittkort [kreditkoort]
bill/coin	seddel [zeddel]/mynt [münt]

HEALTH

doctor/dentist/	lege [legg-e]/tannlege [tannlegg-e]/
paediatrician	barnelege [baan-e-legg-e]
hospital/emergency clinic	sykehus [sük-e-hüs/legevakt [legg-e-vakt]
fever/pain	feber [fayber]/smerter [smairter]
diarrhoea/nausea	diaré [deearay]/kvalme [kvalm-e]
pain reliever/	smertestillende [smairt-e-stillend-e]/
tablet	tablett [tablett]

POST, TELECOMMUNICATIONS & MEDIA

stamp/postcard	frimerke [freemairk-e]/postkort [postkort]
I need a landline phone card/	Jeg trenger et telefonkort/kontantkort
prepaid card for my -mobile	[yayi trenger ett telefonkort/kontantkort]
Where can I find internet access?	Hvor er nærmeste internettilgang?
	[voor er nairmest-e internetttilgang]
Do I need a special area code?	Må jeg slå et spesielt nummer først?
	[mo yayi shlo ett speseelt nummer ferst]
dial/	slå et nummer [shlo ett nummer]/
connection/engaged	linje [liny-e]/opptatt [upptatt]
internet connection/wifi	internettilkobling [internett-tilkoblin]

LEISURE, SPORTS & BEACH

(rescue) hut/avalanche	hytte [hütt-e]/ras [raz]
cable car/chair lift	taubane [towbaan-e]/stolheis [stoolhice]
low tide/high tide/	fjære [fyair-e]/flo [floo]/
current	strøm [strerm]
beach/bathing beach	strand [stran]/sjøbad [sherbad]

NUMBERS

0	null [nüll]	10	ti [tee]
1	en [ayn]	11	elleve [ellv-e]
2	to [too]	12	tolv [toll]
3	tre [tre]	20	tjue/tyve [chü-e/tü-ve]
4	fire [feer-e]	100	hundre [hün-dre]
5	fem [fem]	200	tohundre [toohün-dre]
6	seks [zeks]	1000	ettusen [ettüsen]
7	sju/syv [shü/züv]	2000	totusen [tootüsen]
8	åtte [ott-e]	½	en halv [ayn hal]
9	ni [nee]	¼	en kvart [ayn kvart]

NOTES

FOR YOUR NEXT HOLIDAY ...

MARCO POLO TRAVEL GUIDES

ALGARVE

AMSTERDAM

BARCELONA

BERLIN

BUDAPEST

CORFU

DUBROVNIK &
  DALMATIAN COAST

DUBAI

EDINBURGH

FINLAND

FLORENCE

FLORIDA

FRENCH RIVIERA
  NICE, CANNES &
  MONACO

IRELAND

KOS

LAKE GARDA

LANZAROTE

LONDON

MADEIRA
  PORTO SANTO

MALLORCA

MALTA
  GOZO

NEW YORK

NORWAY

PARIS

RHODES

ROME

SAN FRANCISCO

STOCKHOLM

THAILAND

VENICE

MARCO POLO

With ROAD ATLAS & PULL-OUT MAP

LAKE GARDA

TE BALDO WITH MOUNTAIN BIKE
ar in Malcesine takes bikes too

SSES" IN SALÒ
hocolate "Ducetti"

Travel with
Insider Tips

MARCO POLO

With STREET ATLAS & PULL-OUT MAP

NEW YORK

NDOWS, WILD FLOWERS AND SKYSCRAPERS
is chic: the High Line in Chelsea

IL ON CLOUD NINE
top bar at 230 Fifth Street

Travel with
Insider Tips

MARCO POLO

With ROAD ATLAS & PULL-OUT MAP

FRENCH RIVIERA
NICE, CANNES & MONACO

SPECTACULAR GRAND CANYON DU VERDON
Breath-taking scenery that takes some beating

SNIFFING THE AIR
The perfume manufacturers of Grasse

Travel with
Insider Tips

www.marcopolouk.com

MARCO POLO

With STREET ATLAS & PULL-OUT MAP

BERLIN

A STUNNING ISLAND JUST FOR ART
Showcasing treasures from around the world

STAY COOL AT NIGHT
scene sets the trend

Travel with
Insider Tips

MARCO POLO

With ROAD ATLAS & PULL-OUT MAP

ALLORCA

AN FLAIR IN THE MEDITERRANEAN
Mallorca's most beautiful beach

. IN" CROWD MEET
enda in Deia

Travel with
Insider Tips

www.marcopolouk.com

- PACKED WITH INSIDER TIPS
- BEST WALKS AND TOURS
- FULL-COLOUR PULL-OUT MAP
  AND STREET ATLAS

ROAD ATLAS

The green line ▬ indicates the Trips & Tours (p. 100-105).
The blue line ▬ indicates the Perfect Route (p. 30–31).

All tours are also marked on the pull-out map

Exploring Norway

The map on the back cover shows how the area has been sub-divided

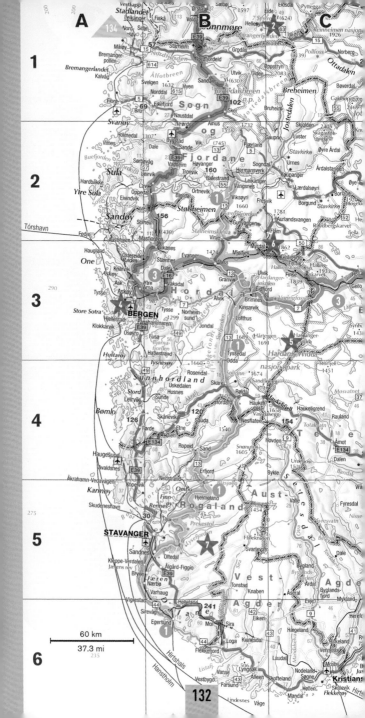

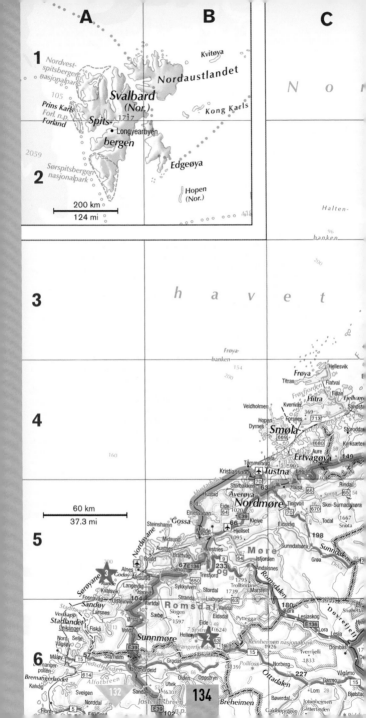

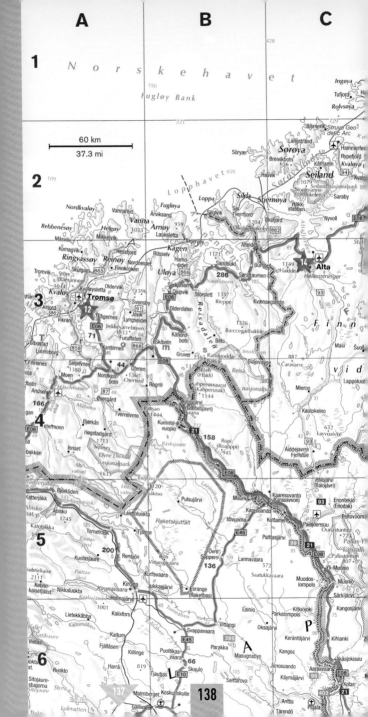

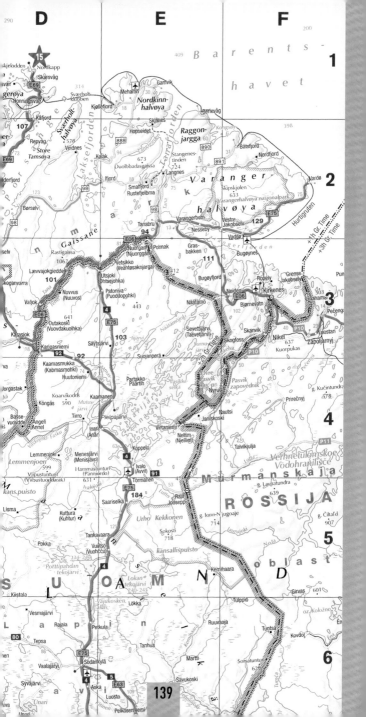

KEY TO ROAD ATLAS

Highway, multilane divided road - under construction Autobahn, mehrspurige Straße - in Bau		Autoroute, route à plusieurs voies - en construction Autosnelweg, weg met meer rijstroken - in aanleg
Trunk road - under construction Fernverkehrsstraße - in Bau		Route à grande circulation - en construction Weg voor interlokaal verkeer - in aanleg
Principal highway Hauptstraße		Route principale Hoofdweg
Secondary road Nebenstraße		Route secondaire Overige verharde wegen
Practicable road, track Fahrweg, Piste		Chemin carrossable, piste Weg, piste
Road numbering Straßennummerierung	E20 11 70 26	Numérotage des routes Wegnummering
Distances in kilometers Entfernungen in Kilometer	259 130　129	Distances en kilomètres Afstand in kilometers
Height in meters - Pass Höhe in Meter - Pass	1365 •	Altitude en mètres - Col Hoogte in meters - Pas
Railway - Railway ferry Eisenbahn - Eisenbahnfähre		Chemin de fer - Ferry-boat Spoorweg - Spoorpont
Car ferry - Shipping route Autofähre - Schifffahrtslinie		Bac autos - Ligne maritime Autoveer - Scheepvaartlijn
Major international airport - Airport Wichtiger internationaler Flughafen - Flughafen	✈ ✈	Aéroport importante international - Aéroport Belangrijke internationale luchthaven - Luchthaven
International boundary - Province boundary Internationale Grenze - Provinzgrenze		Frontière internationale - Limite de Province Internationale grens - Provinciale grens
Undefined boundary Unbestimmte Grenze		Frontière d'Etat non définie Rijksgrens onbepaalt
Time zone boundary Zeitzonengrenze	-4h Greenwich Time -3h Greenwich Time	Limite de fuseau horaire Tijdzone-grens
National capital Hauptstadt eines souveränen Staates	**OSLO**	Capitale nationale Hoofdstad van een souvereine staat
Federal capital Hauptstadt eines Bundesstaates	**Nancy**	Capitale d'un état fédéral Hoofdstad van een deelstat
Restricted area Sperrgebiet		Zone interdite Verboden gebied
National park Nationalpark		Parc national Nationaal park
Ancient monument Antikes Baudenkmal	∴	Monument antiques Antiek monument
Interesting cultural monument Sehenswertes Kulturdenkmal	* Chambord	Monument culturel interéssant Bezienswaardig cultuurmonument
Interesting natural monument Sehenswertes Naturdenkmal	* Gorges du Tarn	Monument naturel interéssant Bezienswaardig natuurmonument
Well Brunnen	⌣	Puits Bron
Trips & tours Ausflüge & Touren		Excursions & tours Uitstapjes & tours
Perfect route Perfekte Route		Itinéraire idéal Perfecte route
MARCO POLO Highlight	★1	MARCO POLO Highlight

INDEX

This index lists all places and sights featured in this guide.
Numbers in bold indicate a main entry, F refers to the front flap

WRITE TO US

e-mail: info@marcopologuides.co.uk

Did you have a great holiday?
Is there something on your mind?
Whatever it is, let us know!
Whether you want to praise, alert us
to errors or give us a personal tip –
MARCO POLO would be pleased to
hear from you.
We do everything we can to provide the
very latest information for your trip.

Nevertheless, despite all of our authors'
thorough research, errors can creep in.
MARCO POLO does not accept any
liability for this. Please contact us by
e-mail or post.

MARCO POLO Travel Publishing Ltd
Pinewood, Chineham Business Park
Crockford Lane, Chineham
Basingstoke, Hampshire RG24 8AL
United Kingdom

PICTURE CREDITS
Cover photograph: Getty Images: Harding (Fishing village on the Lofoten islands)
Chromorange (104/105); DuMont Bildarchiv (66); DuMont Bildarchiv: Modrow (15, 23, 30 bottom, 68, 76, 84, 98, 112, 118 top), Nowak (6, 7, 38), Spitta (41, 57, 118 bottom); Martin Ernstsen (16 top); S. Gabriel (82); Getty Images: Harding (1 top); Huber: Bernhart (58), Damm (18/19), Gräfenhain (front flap left, 2 centre top, 2 centre bottom, 2 bottom, 3 centre, 3 bottom, 9, 10/11, 32/33, 37, 44, 46/47, 48/49, 53, 60/61, 64/65, 80/81, 86/87, 100/101, 113, 119, 141), Huber (12, 34, 43), Mezzanotte (28, 28/29, 114, 114/115), Sharpe (96/97), Zachlod (130/131); Per Arne R. Juvang (16 centre); J.-U. Kumpch (1 bottom); Laif: Aurora (21), Babovic (88, 102), Boisvieux (72), Le Figaro Magazine (55), Galli (62, 91), Handl (2 top, 5, 26 right), Vaisse (30 top); Look: age Fotostock (92/93), Greune (3 top, 70/71, 110/111), Leue (50), van Groan (109); Lyngen Lodge AS: Graham Austick (17 bottom); mauritius images: AGE (4, 8, 106/107), Cubolimages (26 left), Loken (74/75, 94), Nordic Photos (108); moods of norway (16 bottom); C. Nowak (27, 29, 115); Opitz (24/25); Steve Røyset (17 top); J. Seelhoff (52); vario images: imagebroker (79)

1st Edition 2012
Worldwide Distribution: Marco Polo Travel Publishing Ltd, Pinewood, Chineham Business Park,
Crockford Lane, Basingstoke, Hampshire RG24 8AL, United Kingdom. Email: sales@marcopolouk.com
© MAIRDUMONT GmbH & Co. KG, Ostfildern
Chief editors: Michaela Lienemann (concept, managing editor), Marion Zorn (concept, text editor)
Author: Jens-Uwe Kumpch; Redaktion: Corinna Walkenhorst
Programme supervision: Ann-Katrin Kutzner, Nikolai Michaelis, Silwen Randebrock
Picture editor: Barbara Schmid, Gabriele Forst (management)
What's hot: wunder media, Munich
Cartography road atlas: © MAIRDUMONT, Ostfildern
Cartography pull-out map: © MAIRDUMONT, Ostfildern
Design: milchhof : atelier, Berlin;
Front cover, pull-out map cover, page 1: factor product munich
Translated from German by Robert McInnes; editor of the English edition: Christopher Wynne
Phrase book in cooperation with Ernst Klett Sprachen GmbH, Stuttgart, Editorial by Pons Wörterbücher
All rights reserved. No part of this book may be reproduced, stored in a retrieval system or transmitted in any
form or by any means (electronic, mechanical, photocopying, recording or otherwise) without prior written
permission from the publisher.
Printed in Germany on non-chlorine bleached paper

DOS & DON'TS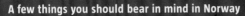

A few things you should bear in mind in Norway

DON'T IGNORE GOOD ADVICE

Norwegians are rather reserved and avoid actively interfering with their guests' plans. However, if someone who knows the place even hints that the weather might change and that it could be better to make your hike or fishing trip shorter rather than longer, accept this a being well-meant advice – and follow it.

DO SAY 'THANK-YOU' FOR EVERYTHING

The little word *takk* is the basis for all politeness and is often a door op... The Norwegians even thank you ... ask how they are. But, they nev... 'thanks for everything' – *takk f...* That is reserved for tombstones, v... ribbons and obituaries. The Norw... are much more precise about thar... after a meal *takk for matten*, a... pleasant evening *takk for i kveld* a... the last get-together *takk for sist...*

DON'T OFFER SPIRITS

In a country where drinks are so e... sive, it is a great temptation to ... gain favour through a bottle of w... even hard liquor. However, that ca... ily backfire. Especially in the sout... west, many people prefer to stay ... from alcohol and find it rather ... tionable if wine or schnapps is of...

DON'T GET IMPATIENT

Norwegians do not push and shove. There is a widespread saying in the country *ting tar tid* (all good things take time) and this applies to road construction just as it does to service in shops. This is different with beer. It is tapped with very little gas and your glass will be full in less than 15 seconds – and you have to pay immediately!

DON'T RISK A TRAFFIC FINE

There are speed controls everywhere. The lowest fine is 600 NOK and it will cost you almost three times that (1600 NOK if you travel more than ... km ... ... headlights ... ... away from your ... ... Don't drink and drive, the ... ... With more than 2 per ... ... sand alcohol in your blood ... ... offence, you may ... ... you will lose your licence, ... are fined and the authorities in ... ... me country informed.

DON'T ...

Take the export regulations ... ... (see 'Travel Tips'). The ... ... in the fjords are endanger... ... ... have an ... into proble... ... ... trailer also disgruntles the locals.